Cambridge Barber Shop Tales

Cambridge Barber Shop Tales

F. T. Unwin

© F. T. Unwin, 1989
First Published in Great Britain, 1989

ISBN 0 9512545 2 9
Published by F. T. Unwin, 9 Cockcroft Place, Cambridge
Tel: Cambridge (0223) 352438

Typeset, printed and bound by
The Burlington Press (Cambridge) Limited,
Foxton, Cambridge CB2 6SW
Tel: Cambridge (0223) 870266

PREFACE

This year the Author celebrates 45 years of door-to-door visitation, in the role of Brushman, Milkman, Colporteur, Provident Man, and current book-selling. In his new book, Mr Unwin gives readers the benefit of those years, by a research into the Barbers of Cambridge, and their tales of the characters who crossed the threshold into their little shops from 1929 to present day. Ladies hairdressers are included in this true picture of "Cambridge Barber Shop Tales"

"Widows harass me to find them a husband, as do the opposite spouse crave of my indulgence to find them a merry widow. They beseech me to write love letters and make arrangements for them to meet. My little shop is a powerhouse of love, I have wigs to transform bald men into swashbuckling romeos, and beautiful wigs for the ladies, turning them into Gainsborough beauties to capture the men's hearts.

I am a factotum for surgeons, dentists, doctors and psychologists. In my cupboard I hold lancets, keep leeches, to lower the blood pressure of lecherous old men; all tricks of the trade for a quality barber. I am the hub of this town. I feel the pulse of all inhabitants, and yet, although they crave of my out-pourings of good advice, when they enter my shop I treat them like Lords. I hot towel their heavily jowled cheeks, pomade their false hair and brush down the evidence of their wanton meanderings.

For the ladies I do likewise, arrange their hair in accordance with the beaus they desire, but I distance myself from their flirtations. They trust me implicitly, as though I'm a mere chaperon – that way, I never lose a customer, but have many temptations that beset me!"

The Author really lifts the lid off a Barber's Shop! A host of local barbers; J. Cartwright, A. Scott, Len Tibbs, Leslie Neal, Chatty Collins, Tip-Toes Harrison, "Prizzy Borsky", Happy Ann Barrett, Miss Pink, and many more, make this book, a unique, and delightful read!

CONTENTS

CHAPTER 1

Cambridge Barber Shop Tales

Doric Street, reminded Pimbo of Casey Court, a street straight out of the comic 'Funny Wonder'. Washing hanging on anything resembling a line, stray cats with their heads buried in empty salmon tins, mothers bawling at dawdling children, returning from shopping expeditions with ready-made dinners for hungry husbands.

At that period Pimbo was living in Staffordshire Street, but was a little out of his area in that Doric Street was situated in what was called the Catholic zone; anyone living within the sound of the resonant Catholic-church bells, was instantly dubbed a 'Doricney'. New Town was the name given to embrace Union Road, Cambridge Place, and Bentick Street and Coronation Street. As Ronnie Witt was saying "You've got to change your image Pimbo, before you join our gang. You're too much of a goody-goody-goody, this work-house stuff, you being illegitimate and T.B. ridden, is old hat. Roy Mountford, our leader, wants red-blood in his gang – another thing, Pimbo, you knocking about with this Jenny gal, Roy won't stand for it – do you *really* want to join?"

Pimbo blinked. Since Jack Peachy from Smart's Row had moved out of the East Road district, things had been very quiet. Jack's 'Black-Hand' gang had ruled the neighbourhood; now, Roy Mountford, with his pal Bobby Lucus, had set their sights further afield, with the idea of forming one large outfit which would ultimately rule the East Road Kingdom, taking in the New Town area as well.

It was a little unfair, he thought, his being called a goody-goody, just because he went to the Sally Army as a child. After all, *he* didn't call Ronnie a baddy-baddy, because he didn't join the S.A.

Ronnie was studying Pimbo intently. "Another thing, Pimbo, Roy's going to alter things. We're all going on twelve now, knocking doors and running away's small fry. We're going to get uniforms, like the Boy's Brigade, but we'll be our own bosses."

"Where's the money coming from Ronnie?" asked Pimbo.

"Roy said, we've got to earn it. You know that film 'Boys Town' – well Spencer Tracy took a whole lot of kids and made something out of them. He didn't take away their spirit, but he put it to a better use."

"But, Roy thinks I'm a goody-goody, how come he'll take me?"

Ronnie was having none of Pimbo's bleating. "We meet tonight in St Matthew's playground, opposite the church; we'll have to climb over the gate so don't let Wardy the window cleaner cop you, he lives right opposite the gate."

Roy Mountford, was a good looking, fair-haired youngster, approaching thirteen magical years. Living in Sturton Street had afforded him a good look into the calibre of boys suited to become members of his gang. By a system of elimination he had whittled his selection down to six boys, over and above the members of his own gang – Pimbo, of course, being one for selection.

"It's like this!" Roy was saying, viewing the huddled up bunch of lads that Ronnie Witt had mustered into the corner of St Matthew's school playground.

"Joining my gang, is going to be beneficial to the lot of you; you can tell your mums that! It's not going to be the ordinary run-of-the-mill circus, smashed windows, or pulling little girls pigtails." Roy gave his audience time for his words to sink in, then went on.

"My dad's friendly with Mr Gaskell the probation officer. *He* told my dad that gangs are good for boys. It teaches boys to identify themselves, it gives confidence to the shy ones, and affords a kind of mob rule, which demands loyalty – but, girls are out." The young leader stared across at Pimbo.

"They tell me you have a little popsy called Jenny. They tell me, too, that you have done quite a bit in the Barnwell area. I reckon you could make a go with me – that is, without Jenny! You don't read about Huckleberry Finn tagging along with girls; where, too, would Oliver Twist have got, with a popsy dragging at his heels?"

Pimbo's face reddened, as he felt the stare of the boys on him. He dearly would love to join Roy's gang. Roy went to the Central school, he knew what he was talking about. Times, too, were changing. People were moving out of the slums, and into better houses, it was up-market, that was the reason for Roy's new gang, he wanted an up-market gang, to do different things.

"What are you going to call the new gang?" came a small voice from the back of the bunch, (evidently trying out an antidote for his shyness). It gave Pimbo a little time to answer Roy's question.

"'Red Hand Gang', 'Black Hand Gang' they're all out" replied Roy. 'The Sturtownians', this name embraces our own locality, and brings in an element of New Town, the 'Townians' covers that – any objections, bring up at the next meeting – I want to hear Pimbo's verdict on ditching Jenny"

Pimbo had got to deep reckoning. Jenny, at the moment, was recuperating from her attack of Scarlet Fever. It could be several months before she could resume her usual active relationship of long walks, and almost grown-up conversations with him. But in no way was he going to ditch his Jenny!

"They say, that behind every succesful man is a loyal wife, or sweetheart. I can't ditch Jenny. You say the gang will teach us loyalty, well, Jenny has helped me so far to get within a whisker of becoming one of your gang members, why not put it to a vote – I promise that my allegiance to the Sturtownians, would in no way be hindered by my friendship with someone who has been a friend of mine for many years!"

Roy stared at Pimbo, half in admiration, and half in frustration, that his leadership had been a teeny bit challenged. He studied the faces of the boys, they told him that Pimbo was one of them. "A show of hands for Pimbo's acceptance in the gang!" he said quickly, knowing full well that every hand was one in favour of Pimbo.

The next meeting was to decide a full programme for the coming winter months.

On his next visit to Jenny, Pimbo found her in good spirits. Her recuperation was going well and he was able to relate to her the business concerning joining the new gang. Jenny seemed always, two years ahead of her boyfriend when it came to maturity and good old common sense. She pointed out that in two years time, Pimbo would be thinking about getting a regular job. His paper round and part-time exploits with Mr Neal, the tailor, were of little bearing toward the time when both might be thinking of getting married.

"Boys, of course gave little thought to what might be in a girls' mind concerning settling down," she half scolded her boyfriend.

"But, you're a girl" said Pimbo a trifle crestfallen, "a boy's got to have an outlet. You don't play sport, all you do is sit and think about getting married. Take my mum she's got nothing, bless her, for all her bottom-drawer scheming, and scrimping – well, she might as well have had a more relaxed childhood. Then, you take the boys in the Great War, how do you think they went straight from home to fight such a bitter war, *because* they had joined gangs like me, *that's* why! They knew what adventure was, they took chances, they were used to mucking in together!"

Jenny smiled "All right then, all I think about is our getting married one day – and you? You think about preparing for war. I reckon my thoughts are the best Pimbo! But you've alway been a go-getter, I know you'll make a good husband, but I guess you'll *have* to go through a gang's apprenticeship, maybe it'll prepare you for something, besides war!"

"Pimbo and Jenny are two old fuddy-duddies", Roy Mountford was speaking to Ronnie Witt after the boys had left the meeting. "Far too old for their years, I'd say. Been to too many welfare meetings well meaning spinsters put funny ideas into their heads – big words, and all that Pimbo has always been a bit of a bookworm!"

Ronnie, nodded. "I'll tell you what, let's put Pimbo through a test. Your new programme needs new ideas, what about putting him in touch with Curly Northfield. Since we accidently broke his kitchen window with a cricket ball, Curly's turned his back on us. We could use him, he knows every nook and cranny in Cambridge but it seems all his know-how now lies buried under broken glass – let's send Pimbo round as a sort of peace-offering; maybe a new face might do the trick?"

Curly Northfield was, indeed, all they had cracked him up to be. His dad once ran a newspaper shop on East Road, almost opposite Staffordshire Street. Curly had delivered newspapers, taken betting slips, and hob-nobbed with both well-to-do and the poor. But, above all, Curly had a heart of gold. He shopped for pensioners too frail to take to the streets, did odd jobs about their homes such as unblocking drains, repairing leaks to the dilapidated roofs and even visited the sick in hospital.

Also, Curly was a boy at heart, what Hiawatha had done for the naturist, Curly had done for the humanist; he loved people, and usually, they loved him!

Pimbo, accepting the new gang's challenge made his may to Curly's home, in a little side street running parallel to Hooper Street, off Mill Road.

Mr Northfield, recognised Pimbo immediately. "You're Tom King's old boy. If you turn out half as good as your dad – you'll do! What brings you round to see me? – the kids, round here take none too kindly to my taking offence at their breaking my window, and to think how many panes of glass I've put in for the pensioners around here?"

Pimbo related to Curly how Roy had ideas of forming a new gang. Of how the current film 'Boy's Town' had gripped the lads of the neighbourhood, turning them from vandals into boys with a desire to amount to something better than street urchins. Mickey Rooney, unwittingly, had done a power of good for the lads and Roy Mountford felt capable of holding the reins in this new surge of citizenship.

Curly smiled. "A far cry from tying tin cans on to cats tails, blowing up frogs, letting down cycle tyres. Boy, I've done the lot in my time but as you get older, you become wiser. Do you know, boy, my first job was calling out names to a little old lady who lived in Abbey Terrace. We called her 'Old Witch'. She was always in black, with a kind of shawl draped around her shoulders. No one seemed to know much about her, she left her tiny one-up-one-down early morning, and returned late in the evening. After she died I found that her journeys were to look after her only grand-daughter, whose father had been killed in the Great War. The mother had to go out to work to support her child; the old lady wore black from the day news had come, concerning her son's death from enemy action. Arthritis had accounted for her reason for wearing the shawl!"

After a lengthy conversation about how best to turn the new gang into something positive, Curley came up with the following idea. An old man he once knew, living in Gas Lane, next door to Wheatley's scrap yard, had a back yard which overlooked the piles of discarded junk, that, seemingly would find its way on to the 'tip' in Coldham's Lane. 'Wally', (Curly never got around to finding out his surname) would amuse himself in the long summer evenings, by going through the cluster of yellowed newspaper and magazines, left lying around the scrap-yard.

Glancing up at Pimbo's earnest little face, Curly pushed on further into the plan.

Wally, one night came across a newspaper snip-pet concerning how in Canada, workmen, digging on a new building site unearthed a jar containing the ins and outs of domestic life, the price of commodities, and how people got on with each other in those far off days, of some fifty years since, the note paper had been carefully sealed in a kind of waxed envelope, and retained most of the written words. It was meant to be a kind of Time Capsule.

"Well!" said Pimbo, wide eyed "what next?"

"Some time ago, a friend to whom Wally had shown the snippet of news decided on doing one himself. Going through his deceased mother's old trunk he'd come across many such items as shown in the Canadian time capsule (actually going back even beyond the years of the original find). Wally told me that the chappie actually showed him the finished article, but wouldn't disclose the where-abouts of the hidden document!"

Curly sighed. "But now, both Wally and the old fellow, by the name of Tom Banks, had died – but Tom's house still exists, derelict and run-down with a condemned notice upon it. I wonder if your new gang could earn their wings by going through the old place like a fine tooth comb; maybe, the capsule thing is still there. What a smashing boost for the boys to cut their teeth on?"

"But, why haven't *you* done anything about it, not like you to miss out?" queried Pimbo.

"Old Tom died just three weeks ago. His house never was of great shakes. He lived alone, except for three cats, maybe, I wanted him to rest a little longer, sort of dignity like. I've had the Time Capsule lark on my mind ever since, or I wouldn't have told you about it!"

"Where's the house? Do you think we could get in without too many prying eyes? Won't it be boarded up against tramps getting in? It's a wizard idea, Roy will go for it like a ton of bricks?"

Pimbo could hardly get his words out quickly enough.

"The house is at the bottom of the entrance to Chatty Collins' barber shop, the same place where East Road School girls hold their cookery classes. It goes down into a dip, and when it rains, it's a proper quagmire, that's why the place has been neglected for years. If we choose a wet day, no-one's likely to bother us, some people call it 'The Hole' – see what I mean?"

"And another thing" added Curly "this little project could do your gang a lot of good, should our search of the house reveal new disclosures, there are a lot of business men in this town, who would put a bit of money into the gang's coffer – your new uniforms could be paid for!"

"Suppose we find nothing?" asked Pimbo.

Curly was cross. "So you're a new gang, eh? Want to be up-market; want to get away from the old tags, create a new image – my boy, you've got a lot to learn. I've been doing all the things your old gang's been up to. You know what? – they're not worth a frazzle. People in the street laugh at 'em. "Suppose we find nothing" eh! Well, what of it. Suppose the great explorers went about their work in such like minds. Come off it Pimbo, no wonder Roy Mountford thinks you lack real guts. Oh, I've heard all about it, I know why you're here, too, you're on a test Pimbo – but I'm not going to be unkind. Go back and tell Roy that I'll meet the gang after the first rainy session from now, and–"

Curly, paused as he watched Pimbo's downcast face as he was about to leave.

A grand shot of the early pioneers of the Hairdressers Federation. At the rear are, Mr Green, Mr Cartwright, Mr Harrison. (See if you can pick out the unnamed!). Front row, the Mathews brothers.

"In my book, you've passed the test with flying colours; any boy would have asked the same question. Tell Roy, that I expect to see you in the gang chosen to search Bank's place, and he's got my full support!"

Pimbo went away in good spirits. On the way back to Roy he couldn't help but wonder why it was that Curly, a grown man, could fall so readily into a boys' adventure. They say all men are boys at heart – and never grow up. Maybe, the gang might put Curly's name into a capsule of their own – then, he would stay young for ever!

CHAPTER 2

The New Plan

At the gang's next meeting Pimbo found that Roy
had installed three new members into the Sturtownians, they were: Jack Fenning with his two
brothers, and B.O. Canwell, an interloper, as was
Pimbo, from another area. Jack lived almost next
door to St Paul's Institute, an edifice, that did
sterling work for the underprivileged and out-of-
work, also providing lantern-slide lectures, taking
the New Town residents out of their meagre
surroundings into the sunshine and gaiety of
magical overseas islands. This was achieved by
joining in with St Paul's church ministers, who
supplied after service lantern shows, attracting
audiences from a widely spread spectrum of Cambridge.

Roy pointed out to the gang, that as St
Swithin's was inside a week of its allotted forty
days of prophesied rain, and so far, had kept up to
its reputation, the time was, indeed ripe, for the
boys to carry out their search for the so-called

capsule in Tom Banks, derelict cottage. Muddy
conditions would keep away builders bent on
pulling down the condemned building.

To Pimbo's joy, the gang leader had chosen him,
along with Ronnie Witt, and the Fenning
brothers, to complete the six adventurers to take
on the task of finding the hoped for time capsule.

It was, fortunately, an over-cast night with
intermittent rain helping to keep out prying eyes.
Pimbo's sixpenny Woolworth torch, complete with
battery, was doing good work in probing for gaps
in the shuttered up windows, while Roy and the
rest were trying out the front of the cottage.
Pimbo, after a short time, was able to pry away a
loose slat covering the window which, after re-
moval, gave easy access to the remainder of the
boarding.

Speeding around to the front of the house
Pimbo was able to lead the gang to where entry
could be made without undue attention from
passers-by in the East Road area, which overlooked. The 'Hole'.

There was no problem from broken glass. Minor
gangs from Burleigh-Back-Lane, had made a
thorough job of smashing every pane in the rot-
ting window frames. Pimbo realised the reason for
Roy's up-market ideas for his new formation –
maybe, the sound of breaking glass, was an antidote to weaken the frustrations of boys, whose
parents spent most of their time slanging each
other off – but, surely, there had to be another
way?

Inside the house, the boys split up, with Roy,
Ronnie and Jack Fenning taking the downstair

room, and Pimbo with the two brothers to search the bedroom.

Pimbo found several Reckitt's Blue tablets, along with an old packet of Robin starch and some Imp firelighters. Apparently old Tom, a widower for many years, had tried his hand at washing a few 'smalls' although for the life of him Pimbo couldn't fathom out Tom's use for Robin's Starch. The 'Imp' firelighters empty packet prompted Pimbo to scrutinize the old fireplace, which must have been the builders very last grate to be installed in a one-up and one-down dwelling.

The chimney ledge was particularly wide. With the thought of many films he'd seen, showing how at times, loose fire-bricks, had disclosed many a secret, maybe hidden away for years – Pimbo felt diligently the chimney surround.

Deep inside the chimney wall, Pimbo, with heart beating very swiftly, found what he'd hoped he might, a fire-brick which actually had been tampered with to present a ready made miniature vault – inside he found a small tin, which proved to be an old Oxo receptacle.

To his surprise the Oxo tin was unsealed, although over the years the lid had rusted enough to make it difficult to prise open.

Not wishing, in any way, to damage the contents by wrenching the lid open, Pimbo took his find down to Roy and the remainder of the gang. On the way, Pimbo felt how good it was that he had been able to make some kind of discovery. It would stand him in good stead with the leader's rating of his progress.

Roy snatched the tin from his grasp, excitedly.

Taking from his pocket a thin-bladed pocket knife of the Scouting variety, he carefully worked the blade around the inside of the corroded lid. To the awaiting gang's relief, it came away without apparent damage to the unknown contents.

The gang leader, after a careful scrutiny of the tin's contents, which consisted of a few sheets of carefully folded note-paper, yellow with age, looked around at the expectant boys.

"A bit of a let down. Seems old Tom never got around to finishing the project, more of a damp squib than a time capsule. You're a bit of an egg-head, see what you make of it" Roy finished, handing the find over to Pimbo.

Pimbo, hardly went along with the 'egg-head' comment, after all, Roy attended the Central Boys School, having sat a scholarship in order to enter the highly rated school, and he was a year older than Pimbo. Taking the proffered pages he read intently a strange list of categorised books, which must have been on sale a good many years ago, as Pimbo couldn't remember ever seeing even the likes of them, the list read as follows:

Children's Books – Leather Bound

Meade (L.T.) Daddy's Boy. With 8 illustrations. Crown 8VO 3/6

Meade (L.T.) Deb and the Duchess. With 7 illustrations. Crown 8VO 3/6

Meade (L.T.) The Beresford Prize. With 7 illustrations. Crown 8VO 3/6

Meade (L.T.) The House of Surprises. With 7 illustrations Crown 8VO 3/6

Praeger (Rosamund) The Adventures of the Three

Bold Babes A story in pictures. 24 coloured plates. Oblong 4TO 3/6
Praeger (Rosamund) The Further Doings of the Three Bold Babes 3/6
Stevenson (Robert Louis) A Child's Garden of Verses 8VO 5/-
Upton (Florence K and Bertha)The Adventures of Two Dutch Dolls and a 'Golliwogg' Oblong 4TO 6/-
Upton (Florence K and Bertha) The Golliwogg's Bicycle Club. With 31 coloured plates and numerous illustrations. Oblong 4TO 6/-
Upton (Florence K and Bertha) The Golliwogg in War. 31 Coloured plate Oblong 4TO 6/-

While Pimbo was perusing the Oxo tin's contents, Roy briefed the rest of the gang on the rather disappointing result of their evening's work.

"But how on earth could an old chap like Mr Banks get himself tangled up with children's books – he had little or no education – surely time capsules and books are miles away from his style of living?" Jack Fenning was questioning the others.

Pimbo was begining to think on similar lines. But then, take Wally who, in the first place, had started the whole thing off. Those long summer nights, spent by him browsing over the ancient magazines and periodicals, his reading about the Canadian discovery. Who's to know to what lengths the two old men had gone, in order to make something out of their lives. Maybe, they both burned the midnight oil?

Tom had gone as far as looking up his mother's old trunk contents.

Roy, broke his thoughts, "I think Tom Banks never really finished his work. Maybe, he became disillusioned, there's nothing in the contents concerning his mother's belongings, perhaps there was more to come – in any case, the book list might be a mine of information for the experts but for ordinary folk around this area, we've got to think up something more in keeping with every day life!"

Pimbo was puzzled about the whole affair. The fact that for 3/6, leather bound books, with coloured illustrations, written by authors he'd never heard of existed in such times; he would have loved to have seen them, felt them, and read every word. 'The Golligwogg in War' which war? What a lovely title, then too, 'The Golliwogg's Bicycle Club', would it be a penny farthing? or one with wooden wheels?

Also, how could Babes actually be bold? Pimbo reckoned the find *was* extraordinary. In fifty years hence it would be more extraordinary, that's what time capsules were all about. He reckoned that a leather bound book in years hence would cost pounds and pounds. What about the book-binders in those days. How much could they earn by producing a 3/6 book? He pictured some old boss like Scrooge, to be looking over their work, and begrudging every penny paid to them.

Roy was right though! It had been a bit of a let down, the boys had expected something more dramatic, they'd seen their mum's reading Red Star Weekly, with the Corder murders, and the Red Barn intrigue, they undoubtedly wanted blood!

"It's back to Curly!" said Roy suddenly. "He'll put us right, maybe he'll come up with something else, at least we've had a go, and the old notes might prove to be useful to someone – some of the old college dons, may well go bonkers when they feast their eyes on a list of old books! Digging back into the archives is just their cup of tea!"

Curly was in a good mood when the boys visited him in fact, Pimbo felt that the great man was in his most reflective attitude.

Time, he told them, was a most precious commodity. God had given it to the world so He made sure there was enough of it. It could not be turned back, only in memory. Curly told the boys that the time capsule venture *had* been a success. Maybe, Wally and Tom Banks had started off something which the boys might enlarge on. Curly pointed out that one day, rummaging amongst some old papers in his grandmother's house after her demise, he found a shopping list which his granny had used at Barbroke's store on East Road: Matches 2 boxes a penny. Candles 3^d a dozen. A small loaf of bread 2½^d. Beef dripping 6^d a lb. Paraffin 6^d a gallon. Eggs 6^d a dozen.

Roy was getting a trifle impatient as Curly went on. "We want a new project, Mr Northfield! I'll grant you the shopping list has an archaic value. What can you rake up for us, you know, the Tom Banks affair has whetted our appetite – it's got to be on similar lines, our new gang has got to justify its being!"

Curly walked across to a copy of yesterdays evening news. Pointing to a caption, he held the article in front of the boys. 'Local barber, commits suicide. After fifty years of hairdressing in one of the poorest areas of Cambridge, Mr A. Hunt was found dead in his lock-up shop. The police state that no suspicious circumstances were apparent.'

"There's your new project. A dossier on all the barbers servicing the public of this Town. Do you know when I was a boy, a barber's shop had a magical influence on me. From the improvised seat on my first hair-cut, the remarks from the teasing old men customers "You *are* a big boy" "Never even cried – did he Mum?" "Give him a shave while you're at it, Guv!" "Never shave 'til you have to boy, that, what you've got, is only bum-fluff!""

Curly, smiled at the gang's ready acceptance of his proposal. Some time capsule *that* would make. Why, a barber's shop was a meeting place for all the characters of the shop's area. The gossip flowing from mouth-to-mouth. The sporting memories brought back by the eldest of the patrons. Then, too, the répertoire of wonderful stories the barber himself could unfold. A whole history of people's lives, the changes that had taken place over the barber's period of being 'right there among 'em' listening to the ups-and-downs of the working class, the triumphs of getting new jobs, getting married, and the little lad perched on the make-shift chair for his first hair-cut, now, big enough to whisper in the barber's ear for his first condom!

Roy had heard enough "O.K. Curly, you win, I'll change the gang's project to that of finding out the history of the Town's barbers. From what you've told us, we only have to find a Barber Shop

Quartet, and we'll have the historians in a real lather!"

From then on plans were laid; Pimbo was given the task of ferreting out as much data from that doyen of barber's, Mr Scott of 120–121 East Road, which in turn could be, by the extra data collected by the rest of the gang, documented in readiness for a time capsule. Scott's hairdressing salon, managed by Mr H. Scott, with his sons as erstwhile apprentices, was almost an institution, situated in the centre of Barnwell, and patronised by the working-class families of that era. (The young Mr Albert Scott, actually gave Pimbo's mother her last hair-trim). From Mr Scott, Snr, Pimbo gained the following information:

The Cambridge Hairdressers Association was founded in 1914. The members comprised the following:

Mr J. Cartwright. President. Shop site – 74–76 Fitzroy Street.

Mr M. Green. Shop site, 169 East Road.

Mr A. Mathews. Shop site, 152 Mill Road.

Mr F. Mathews. Shop site, 16 Fitzroy Street.

Mr R. H. Lowe. Shop site 57 Kingston Street.

The Committee: H. Scott, H. Ward, V.L. Rolph, H. Mathews, M. Green, S. Beger, J. Gold. (At the time four Mathew brothers were full-time hairdressers.)

A small booklet was issued to each member of the Association, this stipulated the prices to be charged for barbering services. For shaving, minimum charge $1\frac{1}{2}^d$. Hair-cut, Gents 3^d, Boys 2^d. Shampoo 3^d. 6^d constituted the price for a week's shave. Razors ground 6^d.

At the death of a member, a Benefit Dance was usually held. Old records, gave the amount collected on two occasions as £21 and £32 respectively.

The Association held its position with rare dignity. A stern discipline permeated into the standard shown by the barber-shops owned by its members. Outings were arranged to the seaside and other various attractions. A picture (in Mr Scott's possession) showing the Association members on an annual outing, emphasises by the smartly dressed barber, how proud they were to be in a group of professional men.

A General Meeting was held on the first Monday in each month, commencing as late as 9.15pm.

This, no doubt accentuated the fact that the barbers put in long hours. Sunday morning was usually regarded as shaving day. Many labourers went the whole week without a shave, thus presenting various stages of unsightly stubble at the weekend.

Mr Scott gave Pimbo a mine of information. "Nice to know you boys are doing something useful. I knew your old dad – came in here often. Bowler hat, red face, brown boots, with a Derby jacket and breeches. Sunday mornings round here was bedlam. Then, on Saturdays, we got the horses coming from the station, down to Pink's slaughter house. Shouting and bawling from the drovers. I'll tell you now, boy, I had to keep a steady hand on my cut-throat razor!"

Pimbo took in the various lotions, the meticulously laid out rows of various hair-creams. He

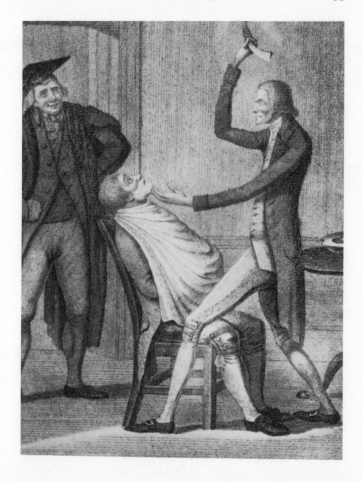

*A very old print, depicting the Dons of King's College,
receiving barbering services in their own quarters!
Published by William Mason, Cambridge.*

reckoned his 2^d tin of Brilliantine would suffice until he was earning more money.

Mr Scott gazed across his son Albert, just home from school, took up a stance behind a newly acquired chair, and began lathering in readiness for the customer's coming shave.

"That's how I started, boy. Lather-boy on a Sunday morning. I hope my lad follows in my trade. I reckon at times I'm philosopher, counsellor, solicitor for the poor and needy. News hound, gossip-monger, yes, I can do my share of gossip. You'll laugh, boy, sometimes I have to put right a sweet heart's quarrel, so you see what a barber's lot is – but I wouldn't trade it for all the tea in China. Oh, I almost forgot, I acted as a book-maker's runner – but keep that quiet, boy!"

Pimbo, left the shop, well satisfied with the result of his first assignment!

CHAPTER 3

Barber Shop Tales Begin!

Delving deeper into the barbers' history, Pimbo found that between 1926–1927 58 barbers were registered with the hairdressers Association. Quite a few scattered around Cambridge were little more than 'Cowboys' – meaning untrained and jumping on the band-waggon of a growing population. One such, known as 'The Flying Barber', used as his wash basin, nothing more than a saucepan. The story goes that the same water and towel functioned for a whole day's work, as this barber did only shaving it meant that customers were dealt with very quickly, thus his nickname 'The Flying Barber'. His establishment was 76 East Road. In those days many Irishmen entered the Town and were billetted in a large hostel type building at the corner of Occupation Road; working hard six days of the week, meant that many be-stubbled workmen were anxious to procure a shave at the cheapest price, irrespective of conditions in the barber's shop. Thus, the Flying

Barber prospered for a while.

A stringent rule of apprenticeship held sway for the bona-fide barber. Lather-boy, was the usual teeth-cutting start for the young would-be barber. The cost of apprenticeship was in the region of £30 per annum this included the ability to set cut-throat razors; singeing and hairstyling.

Pimbo found the Association, on the death of Mr Alf Hunt, of 23 Norfolk Street, had offered not only condolences to his sister, but six members were willing to be coffin-bearers at the funeral – but for some reason or other the next of kin, no doubt through grief, had declined the offer.

A great character considered a 'cowboy' by the proud members of the Association, had a very unusual establishment, in that his 'shop' was so tiny, that only room for the chair was available, which meant that just one customer was able to be dealt with at a time. 'Chinner', Driver, was this worthy's name. His 'shop' on Chesterton Road was next door to a public-house, a narrow passage led to Chinner's shop entrance. The barber was very partial to a quick pint and would nip out leaving his customer, towelled up and bewildered, awaiting service.

Chinner, although very small, was a keen military man, being a member of the local T.A., attending the annual Camp and the usual drill nights at the Drill Hall on East Road. Poor old Chinner, at eighty years of age made a come-back after his first retirement, but although acquiring new premises, his health wouldn't stand any more "Your next, Sir!" – and his retirement became permanent!

Pimbo was very pleased to notice that Len Whitehead's name had been included in the Association's list. Len's shop was at 11 Green Street, a side turning off Trinity Street. During his part-time errand boy sojourn at Mr Neale's, the tailor of Silver Street, Pimbo would often visit Len for a quick hair-do. Len, was a great character, smart in both appearance and quick wit. A boxing enthusiast, Len's shop would have on its walls pictures of the current boxing heroes. Jack 'Kid' Berg, Jimmy Wilde, the 'Phantom with a hammer in his hand'. Jimmy, although of tiny stature and weight, could knock out opponents much bigger than he and most boxing pundits considered Jimmy weight for weight, was the best in the world. As Len would say "The bottle got him in the end".

Mr Whitehead's shop was a veritable entertainments arena, young blades from the nearby college were his regular patrons. They would sit goggle-eyed, as Len related tales of the legendry pugilists. Rumour has it that in a spare room at the rear of his shop, Len would put through their paces, many students, who eventually obtained boxing blues after his tuition.

Len's dark eyes, beautifully groomed hair, with a parting that put to shame many of his balding customers, attracted the ladies, who, would make 'shop' calls for their boy friends' toilet accessories. The barber's professionalism, afforded him a wide reputation, for hair-dressing of the highest order, indeed, Len was a perfect example of the standards laid down by the Hairdresser Association. 11 Green Street, once visited, left a memory of what a good barber's shop should make an effort

to be! Almost opposite Len's establishment was
that of Mr Herbert Cox. Although an excellent
barber, Herbert lacked a little of Len's flamboy-
ancy, but his little shop at 5 Green Street
attracted a steady flow of customers (which carried on for many years).

From one end of the Town, we journey across
Parker's Piece, to Harry Harrison of 60 Norfolk
Street. Harry, a sterling member of the Association, was considered to be the best-dressed barber in the Town. His little shop was opposite the
butcher's shop of Mr Pauley; Harry, besides being
an excellent pianist, ran his own dance band.
Among his other talents was that of being a good
dancer. He was very light of step and when
walking seemed to be floating along on air, which
undoubtedly earned him the nick-name of 'twinkle-toes Harrison'. As with Len Whitehead, Pimbo
had used Harry's barbering talents. Coming back
from unloading a day's work of totting with his
dad Tom King, Pimbo's task was to hold the head
of the pony, whilst Tom popped in for a shave.
Pimbo, often looked on in envy at the friendly
gas-light shining through on a cold day. But dear
old Harry, would send out a drink of hot Oxo for
Pimbo to warm his cockles with.

A small distance away from Harry's shop, on
the opposite side of the road, close by Mr Mott's
baker's shop, was a barber's pole. It became the
subject of much talk in the vicinity, especially in
the barber's establishments, as to whom the pole
belonged. It was fixed to the side of a house at the
bottom end of Norfolk Street, but no one could
remember a barber's shop ever existing on that

specific site.

That's what Pimbo loved about barbers' shops! At the weekend everyone, who, during the week was tied up at work, would meet in the cosy atmosphere of a cut-and-snip establishment. Whilst waiting his turn, Pimbo, ever curious, would listen in to the latest sports news and local gossip. He smiled as a customer left, it would be his turn to be gossiped about. "They say he treats his wife something awful."

"What she ever saw in him I just don't know!" But Pimbo marvelled at the diplomacy of the good barber.

Never a bad word about anyone. Just a nod here, and there, a well timed 'tut-tut' or a shrug of the shoulders, but nothing to pin down the barber on any straying from the standards expected of an Association member.

Another attraction for Pimbo, was watching the barber during slight lulls, sweep up the mass of hair lying at the foot of the chair. It told a good story of the type of customer going through the shop that day. The sleek, fair hair of the youngster having his 'first'. The thick brown hair of the young man on the threshold of a working career. The mixed grey and black of the middle-aged whose conversation contained a slight tinge of cynicism. To the thin 'all grey' of the pensioner, who required little more than a trim and sometimes would ask a kind hearted barber to 'split a packet of five woodbines", although a full packet cost only $2\frac{1}{2}^{d}$.

Switching away from the East Road area, we journey down to Petty Cury. A short distance

away in Market Hill, was the Jewellers Otto
Wherle. Here, Pimbo spent a few years as an
apprentice watch and clock repairer. It was during those years that Baker's, the barber-cum-
tobacconist, had a kind of attraction for the boy.
The main reason was that the shop catered, in the
main, for the better off as opposed to those that
Pimbo had been used to hob-nob with.

Business managers, clerks, representatives in
the hub-bub of trade around the Town. The shop's
entrance was the tobacconist side of the trade, at
the rear was the cosy first-class department of the
hairdressers salon. Prices, too, were a 'cut' above
the East Road barbers, six pence, apparently was
the minimum charge, going up for the the service
of hot-towels and extras. The main extras were of
course, for singeing, styling, shampoos and the
like.

Out of sheer curiosity, Pimbo would save a
tanner just to watch the goings on in such a
high-class establishment, far removed from Irish
drunks, and the $1\frac{1}{2}^d$ and 3^d touches. Usually,
there were four chairs in use, the salon was warm
and cosy in winter, with excellent lighting. 'Sid' or
'Stan', Pimbo could never remember his right
name, was the King-pin of the staff. Always
smiling with an expert flourish of the towel, a
cheery word, and a good knowledge of all sport,
politics, too, he knew more than most; but with a
view to the possibility of offending a customer, he
would end a slightly controversial subject with
"But of course, on the other side of the coin – to be
fair!"

Pimbo noticed that quite a number of 'tips' were

given and the boy wondered how it was, that a customer could spend as much as a 1/- on a service and afford to 'tip' as well? Baker's shop was at 2 Petty Cury.

A little way down from Baker's, was the salon of Robert Alderton, at 13 Petty Cury with an imposing '& Co.' after the name. Alderton's gave service to the most elite of patrons no doubt pulling in many casuals visiting the prestigious Red Lion on Degree-day and other social functions.

Further afield, we come to the small barbering outfit of Harry Foister of 6 Peas Hill. In later years, Pimbo made friends with a certain Harry Young whose mother lived at the premises and Pimbo remembered that to enter the actual salon, one had to push aside bead curtains. The current film at the Kinema, was a serial featuring 'Dr Fu-Manchu', the bead curtains gave Pimbo's imaginative mind a fear that 'Fu-Manchu' might be hiding behind them waiting to pounce. Harry Young, must have completed his apprenticeship at No. 6, because a few years later, Harry opened up on his own in Magdalene Street.

A remarkable twist to this tale is that during the last war 1939–1945 Pimbo, in charge of a gun-site at Wyton Aerodrome, was told that a new cook was on his way down the site. To Pimbo's surprise the cook turned out to be Harry Young, who, red-faced at meeting Pimbo said, "I'm not much of a cook, but I thought I'd give it a go. It's a change from cutting hair!"

Harry, after the war, was to make yet another change. Pimbo met him in the Town wearing a smart blue suit, complete with a bowler hat. The

ex-barber-cum-cook was now a fully-fledged college porter. As Harry pointed out "I'm married
now. The money's not great, but I pick up a few
tips and the job's steady and secure!"

Pimbo reckoned that poor old Harry never
made 'a bomb' at barbering, his heart wasn't
really in it! A nice chap was Harry.

Perusing his so far accomplished dossier of the
history of Cambridge Barbers, Pimbo decided that
the time was ripe to go over the findings with the
Sturtownians. At the subsequent meeting, he
found only three members, Ronnie Witt, and the
Fenning brothers.

"It's all over!" said a doleful Ronnie, "Roy's
called it a day, you'd never believe it, but all the
things he's said about you and Jenny, he's done it
himself, gone and got himself a girl. He offered me
the leadership but I'm not taking it, the gang's
finished, Pimbo, maybe we're all growing up too
quickly!"

"But the project, Ronnie. I thought this was
going to be so big, take us out of the rut of
small-fry, why, what about the time capsule,
everyone was so keen – is that to go by the board?"
Pimbo could hardly restrain himself.

"It's finished, the whole caboozle finished!" the
Fenning brothers nodded their assent. Ronnie
went on. "I suggest you go on with the project,
you're the one for getting it done – good luck
Pimbo!"

Pimbo's next move was to confer with Curly.
The veteran smiled at the boy's story. He told
Pimbo that it had to come, the growing-up stage
can happen overnight. It all comes differently, to

different boys. Some boys, when Dad's out, borrow his razor, they flip over what's nothing more than 'bum-fluff', they can't wait to grow up. Others refuse to go shopping with mum. Girls demand bras, ages before really due, I remember locking the bathroom door for the first-time, Mum said something like "Let me in", but I countered with "I'm not ready!" From that day, Mum understood.

"That's what happened to Roy. Like a caterpillar shedding its cocoon, or whatever they call it. Happens overnight, you've been lucky, you've managed to combine Jenny's affection with your boyhood, but remember, Jenny has been ill for some time, it gave you a chance to moderate the shock, by carrying your daydreams into reality. Besides, Roy's a fine looking boy, some gal was sure to nail him!" On Curly's advice, Pimbo decided to keep on the Cambridge Barbers project. As the wily veteran had pointed out, maybe it might be turned into a book. The time capsule lark would be similar to hiding a light under a bushel, whereas a book would be available to everyone.

Pimbo, before consulting Jenny on the change of plans, decided to ferret out one more barber, or two, which would bring his research up to an amount likely to stimulate Jenny's assistance. Along the way, he'd not been too keen at leaving Jenny out of things. Somehow, he was glad the gang was over. Roy's sudden change, was proof that it could happen to anyone. Maybe, in time to come, passive street gangs would be out. Boys, after a terrible war, would be looking for real excitement. There might still be gangs, but Pimbo reckoned that instead of the old ways, violence, stealing, and vandalism would take place.

The time capsule caper was a step in the right direction, but despite the integrity of the boys desire to do something different, how easily it had all fizzled out. Pimbo intended to see his project out. Spencer Tracy and Micky Rooney wouldn't have given in. After all, it was their film 'Boys Town' that had incited the boys in the first instance! Maybe, he'd call the book 'Barbers' Town', how about that?

Another thing, in 'A Tree Grows in Brooklyn" the hero, Wallace Ford, kept his shaving mug in a private cubicle in the barber's shop. On his death, his broken-hearted little daughter, Polly Ann Garner, fetched it from the kindly barber who gave her Dad an excellent reference. That's what barber's shops were all about, thought Pimbo, Yes, he'd go on!

Pimbo's next on the barbers' list, was J. Prziborsky, the 'Count' of 9 Round Church Street. This gentleman had been court-hairdresser to a Bavarian dynasty. In those days, Russians, due to the many comic-papers depicted all Russians and their like as wearing black capes, sombrero type hats, and usually carrying a bomb at their rear, caused many rumours concerning Mr Prziborsky. One such, that in the bottom of his basement was kept a large bear. This of course, was completely unfounded.

Nothing was ever proved, but around this illustrious barber was an aura of intrigue, which, of course, swept around all areas of Cambridge. Prizzie was an excellent barber, he had in use, two very special electric roller-cum-trimmers, maintained regularly by an electrician friend who lived nearby. He was a cheerful man, very willing to laugh at himself and, apart from the rumours surounding him, he gained a good deal of respect from his clientele. Many of his customers were drawn from the college students, who in those days were up at college to learn about life, in lieu of academics. At that time, Leslie Neal and Freddie Osborne were working with the master-barber. Prizzie's very name, as a Count, attracted the public; in that era, foreign names had to mean something special. Prizzie, owing to building requirements and the like, finally called it a day. Freddie Osborne opened up on his own in Trumpington Street, and Leslie Neal in Mill Road.

Afterwards, as Pimbo passed by on his errand boy's bike, he would give a furtive glance to Prizzie's window, hoping to see the mythical bear being put through his paces by the sturdy little Count with the sharp pointed beard.

Having recorded his newly found data, Pimbo decided to look up Jenny with a view, not only to put her in the picture, but maybe induce her to help out with his project. It would give her something to do, should she just copy his findings into a note book with her neat handwriting!

Jenny was looking more of her old self when Pimbo called. Listening to his explanation about the demise of the newly formed Sturtownians caused a little smile to appear on her still pale face. "It had to happen" she said kindly "things are changing, new ideas, everyone's looking for something different. Do you know in America,

Pimbo, the movie people have just introduced a
film which includes sound. It's called 'Don Juan',
with a musical score in line with the action of the
film. When John Barrymore crosses swords with
Montague Love you actually hear the swishing of
the blades, as soon as the duel is over the
swishing stops – not one swish too many. What
makes it more magic, is that the sound comes
from behind the screen – not from the orchestra
pit!"

Pimbo nodded. "Sort of makes our little games
seem small fry. But the barber's book, I'd like you
to help me with it. Maybe, in years to come, a new
generation would love to read about the old
characters – what about it Jenny?"

*C. Pilson (Interior). Barbers at work showing special rollers
being used (which, were later barred from use). These were
either electrically controlled, or, as in picture hand
manipulated.*

A picture of the oldest working barber in Cambridge. Mr Albert Scott, of East Road.

Taking the written material which Pimbo had laid on the table, Jenny went through its contents. "It's good! You like writing don't you? But I reckon I'm the only one to understand what you've written – I mean, you write so scrawly. I like the idea better than the time capsule, I wouldn't like all your hard work to be buried until we're past and gone!"

"Then, you'll help me, Jenny?"

"Of course, did you ever doubt otherwise I'll copy it all down for you, maybe visit one of your special barber shops – another thing Pimbo, there's a shop in the Town that cuts ladies hair as well as men's. We could sit together as we get our hair trimmed – that'll be another of the changes we're always on about!"

CHAPTER 4

'Chatty' Collins

I was 12 years of age at the time. Jenny said that
if I didn't get a haircut, she wouldn't go out with
me until I did. Up to the age of 10 years, most of
my haircuts were done by a simple method of
placing a basin over my head, then snipping
around the basin with scissors. Most of the kids at
school had the same routine, so I don't feel too
ashamed to attend school after a haircut.

But, at twelve, a boy had pride. Jenny's hair
was always pretty and tied at the back with a
pretty ribbon. Now, boys don't go much on appearance. In those days, no-one looked really smart.
Take 'Just William' for instance, never looked
tidy, did he? Wrestling on wet grass, jumping
ditches, (and falling a foot or two short) doesn't
lend itself to a tidy appearance. So I saved up 2^d
and walked boldly into 'Chatty' Collins hairdressing salon on East Road; almost opposite Gold
Street it was, 56 East Road, R. Collins.

Now I never did know why they called the

barber 'Chatty', some said it was because he rarely washed the towel he placed around the customer's neck; and in accordance with the type of client the barber dealt with, it was possible that fleas were hopping from one meal to another.

The other theory was that Collins talked too much – hence 'Chatty'.

'Chatty' was filling in a racing slip when I entered, a soiled looking copy of the *Sporting Life* lay before him.

"Never back horses boy!" he told me. "It's a mug's game, two can't win. But I'm a fighter against odds so I have a bash, three-penny accumulator boy, that's my limit".

As he was talking, I took in the interior of the shop. The entrance was actually at the side of the shop, three stone steps leading into the shop, with a small window looking out on to East Road. Past the entrance was a steep incline, which ran down into the Girl's Cookery Centre.

'Chatty' had never got up-to-date. A simple wash-basin, with three tide-marks from recent 'shampoos'. No taps, 'Chatty' kept his water in a large jug. A portable mirror, in the shape of an ordinary looking-glass stood before the customer. 'Chatty' had dusted just enough space for a client to see his face.

"Up you get then boy!. A bit small ain't you? I see you've had a basin-cut as some time or other, do you know, boy, some lads come in a bit of pudding still stuck behind their ears – at least you've spared me that!"

I noticed a set of photographs at the side of the mirror. Jack Dempsey caught my eye. 'Chatty' noticed my gaze on the photographs. "Now that fellow Dempsey *was* a good 'un. If he'd gone to his corner straight away from knocking down Tunney, he'd have won the fight, they reckon he must have counted at least twenty, the ref I mean!"

But, Tunney won the return, I pointed out!

'Chatty' was snipping away industriously at my locks, now and again I felt a snatch, and drew my head sharply away. The barber walked across to a drawer next to the wash-basin, and, after testing out two pairs of reserve scissors, chose a pair, throwing the pair he'd been using on me, into a box marked 'Sharpining'. I made no comment on the spelling mistake, as 'Chatty' pointed out the fact that Old Tom, the scissor grinder, hadn't called on him lately. "Good old boy is Tom. Come from the Fens, they say. Got a nice tackle too. Sort of lathe and mobile rub-stone. Fixed the belt and wheel himself, they say. His dad was a sort of blacksmith, then, when the tractors came in, his old dad said 'Tom, my boy, you ain't the marrying sort, what are you now forty, ain't you? Well, I ain't moved out of Manea for forty years, now, I don't want the same to happen to you, I'll set you up with a little contraption, and, instead of people coming to you, you can go out into the highways and byways and visit them. A travelling-grinder they can call you!'"

"So that's what Old Tom's been doing for as long as I can remember, must be touching eighty, if he's a day! He does the butcher's knives, tackles lawn-mowers, goes round the houses, for sharpening scissors and table-knives. Hope nothing happened to him, the only place I know where I can get my stuff sharpened is a place in Christ's Lane, Betts, or some name, next to Ladd's the grocers!"

My hair seemed to be dropping on the floor in bushels; all colours, I'm sure my friend Ginger Sparkes must have been one of Chatty's victims, because a fair chunk of ginger hair mingled with black, brown and grey. I looked across to the wash-basin with its 'tide' marks, I mischievously thought about how they tell the age of trees, by the rings in the centre of the trunk. I reckoned that 'Chatty's' basin must have been a good age, on account of its 'tide' marks.

'Chatty' was at it again! "I used to get a cheeky young chappie in here, name of Pilsworth, lived in Leader's Row. Never used to come in until his hair was down to his shoulders, 'mum said that way, she'd get her money's worth', he'd tell me. Never settled down after he left school, poor kid, couldn't get work, joined the fair, he did. Next thing I heard, some years later, he'd been killed while sitting on the back of one of their trailers. Seemed a waste of a young life!"

I was thinking how may customers old 'Chatty' had in the shop over the years. Mind you, a lot came in just to place bets, but with two-pence a shave, and maybe a sixpenny win, they thought it prudent to pass a bit of trade his way.

"You'd best have a hair wash boy. Your hair's a bit greasy, been putting lard on it again, eh boy? Do you know boy, people must be pretty poor around here. One bloke told me his missus, before going to the flicks, would dab a wet flannel on to the ceiling, wipe of the white mush, and use it as powder on her face!" I knew it was true, I'd seen my mum do it!

'Chatty' placed a dirty looking towel around my shoulders, pulled me up to the wash basin and after pouring a little water overy my head, mixed in a greasy concoction, labelled Altruso. "You know boy, the girls around here never went out on a Friday night. They called it Amami night, on account of the shampoo people. You tell your mates, get a shampoo with me, and put one over on the girls – call it Old Collin's night!"

"Mind you!" the barber went on, "I get a lot of diddi coys during Fair time. They were telling me about one of Thurston's worker's wives. Reckon she had some kind of muscle disease, so each time the Fair came to Cambridge they used to whip here into hospital, don't know where, they sorted out her medicine, then off she went until next time round."

After drying my hair, the barber put on the kettle. "You may as well have a hot drink with me boy, all in the charge. By the way, where did you get the 2^d from?" "Mrs Mahoney in Staffordshire Street" I told him. "Always gets me to fetch her budgie seed. Gets it from French's in bulk, why do you ask?"

While pouring out my tea into a dirty mug, 'Chatty' laughed. "Lots of boys pinch money from the old ladies they run errands for, they don't give right change, then they come in here to buy Woodbines. But they don't get 'em off me!"

It suddenly dawned on me, that the real reason for the barber's nickname was because he *was* 'Chatty' and also he *was* 'Chatty' because of the little fellows that jumped from towel to head. A sort of double-barrelled nickname Chatty-Chatty, sounded classy. He was a little man, kind looking, seemed to have seen so much life go through his seedy little shop that it almost came to saturation point.

'Chatty' couldn't have seen the sun go down, or come up. Day in, day out, he was in the shop, even on Sunday mornings he was open. His *Sporting Life* gave out the names of the horses he and his customers backed. But no galloping hooves for 'Chatty', no jockey's colours flashing by the winning post, no sight of the undulating Newmarket downs. Freddie Fox and Tommy Weston were his heroes, but he only read about it all!

I was reckoning that having been in 'Chatty's' for about half-an-hour, all he would be getting out of me was 2^d. A customer came in, walking up to 'Chatty' he whispered something in the barber's ear who, opening a small cardboard box he'd taken from his scissors' drawer, drew out a small single packet and handed it to his client.

'Chatty' was doing all this in a very hush-hush way.

But he needn't have bothered, I knew all about Durex; boys in the school play-ground talked about all sorts of things – girls, and of course, Durex. What we didn't know, we soon invented.

I asked the barber if he'd ever been to London, wouldn't he like to get away from his same-old-thing, and seek the glamour of the big City?

"Boy, I'm like old Fagin, that chap from Oliver Twist. People come in here, I trim a beard, shave a face, cut a hair, and off they go into the outside world; they all shoot away on some self design, or

other. I just stay here, as I said, waiting like old
Fagin for them to return and tell me all about it,
that's what a barber's shop is – a good old natter!"

He went on. "A chap came in one day, he'd
sampled two-pennyworth of London, wasn't that
impressed! Too busy working to pay the high
rents, the high cost of bus fares, not once was he
able to afford a theatre or cinema visit. He reckoned that he might as well be living anywhere,
another thing he told me was that he rarely got a
goodnight's kip, what with traffic noise and all
that!"

It was pouring with rain, I was in no hurry,
'Chatty' was wiping up the two cups, somehow, we
both seemed to be on the same wavelength. I don't
think the barber had ever been married, he never
talked about it, or about his children.

At school our subject for the week had been
Income Tax. Anxious to enlarge on this, I asked
him if he had to pay income-tax on his earnings?

He almost fell off his chair laughing. "I have two
books, one for myself and one for the tax-man.
Now, I'll tell you straight away, if I paid tax, the
tax the government expects from me, I'd finish up
in the Workhouse, and it would cost them more to
keep me than any tax they could squeeze from me.

Do you know boy, they expect me to pay tax on
tips I never get. You're not likely to tip me are
you? You've had a cup of tea, haircut and wash, all
for two-pence. Why bless you boy, I don't begrudge
it you – but I've still got to pay the rent!"

"Do you feel guilty about keeping two books?" I
asked.

"I'll tell you a story. A chap used to come in, who

peddled laces, lingerie, elastic and knick-knacks, from door to door. One day, he told me he called at quite a big house in Hills Avenue. The gentleman who answered the door, before slamming it shut, raved on about his having to pay over-heads at the shop he ran, the high cost of materials, and it wasn't for him, to be able to sell stuff with no over-heads involved, and no tax to pay, there was "No Sale!"

He didn't know that the chap who told me this story had once been in business himself, and that through ill-health and bad luck, he'd lost every-thing, and was starting on the bottom rung again; he knew all about tax-fiddles, expense accounts, and so-called, elevated at times – overheads! Not everybody was a tax-dodger, but very few people had much to be proud, or scornful, concerning their tax-returns!

"Were you an apprentice before you become a barber?", I asked. "I started as a lather-boy. Hard work, too, I can tell you. Old Mont Ely, from Castle Hill, Cartwright and Scott, all started the same way. Had to, handling a cut-throat razor isn't child's play, it's something you had to be shown. You can't beat a good old cut-throat boy, don't you ever try using one, cut yourself to bits, it's the left hand that does it!"

"How do you manage with four barbers in the same road, does it take away trade?"

"Well, boy, you could say I'm sort of down-market. Me shop ain't much to look at, I've no fancy hot-and-cold facilities, tell you the truth, I ain't much to look at myself. I know what they call me, I'm not daft you know. Now, you tell me, why did you pick me to cut your hair? You could have got to any of the others"

"I reckoned you'd be cheaper, I only had 2^d. Then, I thought, maybe I wouldn't have to wait so long, you wouldn't be as busy as the others!"

'Chatty' smiled. "Now, tell me, have I done a good job? Mind you, it wouldn't have to be much, to beat a pudding-basin cut. You said, too, you mightn't have to wait so long, but, boy, we've been talking for ages?"

"You've done a good job" I said, checking up in the mirror. "I like listening to you, you tell interesting tales, about the income tax, I can use that in my composition at school!"

'Chatty' seemed pleased at my answers. "I'll tell you a joke!" he said.

"Two young men were going to the pictures, as they approached the box-office they realised they only had enough money for an adult and small child. So one picked the other up and carried him to the pay-desk, in his arms, as though he *was* a small child. After a heated discussion, they were both turned away. 'What went wrong?' asked the one masquerading as the small child. The other retorted – 'you fool, you haven't shaved!'"

"Why don't as many people come in your shop as they do the others?" I queried.

"Maybe I get a different class of person. There's a lot of unemployed about here, those in work can afford the extras; toothpaste, gelatine, fancy talc, draw tickets, everything catered for by the big-wigs. I get drifts and drabs, people out of work. But, I get good conversations, about real things. They talk about their grandparents the circus that used to be in Auckland Road. They tell me how they might be lucky to earn a tanner holding a dealer's horse outside a pub, then off they go to see Vesta Tilley at the Workmen's Hall in Fitzroy Street – all for a tanner!"

"What about the money, the others earn more than you?"

"I never did go a bundle on money. It ain't everything boy. I'm knocking seventy, I don't feel too bad, might make it for a few more years if they

Mr W.E. Beattie, 3 Jesus Lane. Celebrated 50 years' service in the same salon. The salon was equipped with just two chairs, plus a loyal assistant who served with his master for many years.

don't pull the place down. Mine wouldn't stand a chance when it comes to a demolition order last one in the row, damp as hell, no light coming in the back room. Another thing, boy class don't mean nothing to me, we're all flesh and bones — you know!"

Just then my pal Ginger Sparkes walked in. "Your mum's shouting for you, wants you to go to the Maypole for six pennyworth of bacon pieces. Here's the sixpence!" he said, as he handed it to me.

'Chatty' gave my hair an extra rub with the towel, then ran a comb down to form a parting. I took it from him, putting in a fresh parting. I always had a lovely parting, just like the film-star Clive Brook. When I could afford it, I bought a 2^d tin of Brilliantine and really plastered it down. Jenny liked it, but mum moaned, said it soiled the pillows.

'Getting to the door, I realised I hadn't paid over my 2^d to 'Chatty'.

My proffered hand was pushed aside. "Have it on me!" he said. Then pushed a small tin of my favourite Brilliantine into my hand.

I realised then that poor old 'Chatty' Collins would never be rich, that is, only in keeping small boys like myself from getting wet on a rainy day. Where Sweeney Todd sent them crashing down into his cellar —

'Chatty' sent them from his shop — happy!

CHAPTER 5

Mr Cartwright

Pimbo's next barber-cum-personality to come under the spotlight was Mr John Cartwright of 25–26 Fitzroy Street. Pimbo had always been attracted to the double-fronted establishment, as the large windows gave an excellent view to all that went on in the shop. The first part of the shop sold tobacco and cigarettes. But the feature which attracted boys of Pimbo's age, was the plentiful display of comic postcards, which, to a "curious" youth, gave a kind of anatomical lecture. It said much for Mr Cartwright's sense of humour because Pimbo could never remember seeing such cards, other than at the seaside, on display anywhere else.

The Barber was a dignified man, ruddy complexion with silver grey hair. He was a great favourite with the ladies because of his love of life and sense of humour. He as an ardent fishing fan being a lifelong member of the Albion Angling Society. Annually, John would have a poster in

J. Cartwright's double fronted shop, Fitzroy Street, with loyal assistant.

his window depicting the coming Fishing Contest, with tickets available from his shop. He was President of the Hairdressers Association and took a keen interest in social events of all kind. Saturday mornings would see a shop full of customers, with John's apprentice lather boys frantically applying the white froth to the stubbled chins.

Many an establishment barber in later years would owe his know-how to the skills and advice to J. Cartwright.

Mr Cartwright married three times. A son and daughter came from the first marriage. Ironically,

his married son died in 1918, with his wife to
follow within a week of her husband's death. The
second marriage produced no children, but the
third made amends by bringing forth eight. A son
from the last marriage is alive today and is a
skilled electrical engineer. Many and varied are
the tales concerning J. Cartwright, but his memory will linger on in the hearts of those who knew
him.

Another barber living in the vicinity was Bill
Kemp. Bill served a 12-year apprenticeship with
that doyen of master-barbers, H. Scott. Mr Kemp
finished up in a shop wedged between E.O.
Brown's tailor shop and Mr Stokes' cafe. Practically opposite was the Workman's club. Bill was a
kind hearted man who took life as a challenge
from one day to another. The death of his mother,
for Bill, was a hard blow to take. Some say that it
started him on the downward trend regarding his
health, although he could always do justice to a
pint of guinness.

The kindly barber was a dedicated man and
seldom left his shop. So much so that on contract-
ing a leg complaint, Bill, instead of resting, carried on against good common-sense. No doubt,
had antibiotics been available in those days Bill,
like his dear sister, would be alive today. But the
malady took him away from his beloved customers and shop at Fitzroy Street.

During Pimbo's effort to turn Jenny into a
barber's research fanatic he had to explain why it
was that people held such a fascination for, what
to her, seemed no more than an ordinary job of
work. Pimbo pointed out that the barber's shop

was a meeting place for customers to pick up the latest gossip. He knew of one old man, who would wait until the shop was almost full, then take up a seat knowing that he would be waiting a very long time – he would relish all the sports talk, while away an hour or two, all for the price of a 1½^d shave, and learn of the death of some of his old school chums.

Pimbo, with his, at times run away imagination, on looking through a barber-shop window, would visualise during a shave, the helpless customer almost gagged with white foam, and a leering barber brandishing an ominous looking cut-throat razor at the customer's throat. To give credibility to his imagination, in a London theatre at that period, Tod Slaughter was appearing in "Sweeny Todd, the demon barber of Fleet Street". This play, not only took in Pimbo's wildest dreams, but had the wicked barber making meat pies out of the hapless patrons, and selling them to the shop next door. Amazingly, many people actually believed that Sweeny Todd existed which, of course, gave all barbers' shops an air of mystery, which no other trading establishment could match.

Add to this the fact that not long since, barbers' were allowed to do blood-letting (apart from shaving) with leeches. In fact, some barbers were looked upon as surgeons; the white coat, air of authority with both cut-throat and scissors, helped a good deal in establishing the false belief. Then too, during a busy session, no-one would notice, that after a whisper-in-the-ear, the barber would supply to a young lad the means of preventing some poor girl being told by a relentless father 'Never darken my doorstep again!' A true prerogative of a barber's shop!

"There is no doubt" Pimbo told an awe-struck Jenny "that barbers hold an esteem in the public-eye, which will never diminish. The fifty-eight Association members around Cambridge Town must never be allowed to sink into obscurity. In years to come new hairdressing salons will spring up, with new technical equipment, but the intimacy of the little barber shops will be missed by many, who once had experienced the pleasure of 'Hair-cut-or shave, Sir?'"

In pursuance of the barbering history of Cambridge, Pimbo next came up with the name of Deafy Webb. This barber kept a shop in Newmarket Road, next the the public house 'The Bird in Hand'. Mr Webb gave the pub's name a comic twist because whilst servicing a customer he would often be seen with 'a pint in hand'.

To get to Deafy's shop entrance one had to mount awkward steps with a low gradient. Slightly inebriated customers coming straight from the pub at closing time, would find it a 'closer shave' than might be expected from the barber himself, in fighting off serious injury from a likely fall down the imposing steps.

Mr Webb eventually moved to a less hazardous locality in Mill Road. His new premises being close to the Corporation Yard, later to be taken over by a cycle-shop.

The barber's move from Newmarket Road, took him away from the midsummer fair diddi coys, who, made life hectic for any barber-shop within easy access from the Common. The Newmarket racing week brought in a good number of louts roaming up and down in the evening looking for trouble.

Pimbo, in his research for enough material to write a book on Cambridge barbers, was very lucky in that, during the course of his different jobs as errand-boy and watch-maker's apprentice, he was able to take in a whole area of the Town, which embraced most of the barbers listed in the Hairdressers Association dossier. His age enabled him to remember the stories and his own meetings with the wonderful old characters.

Pimbo was at an age when boys, approaching puberty, would have almost an obsession about the appearance of their hair. Film stars like Clive Brook, Edmund Lowe, Don Ameche, would have slick parted hair, with the parting standing out like the Milky Way. It was at the opening of the Alma Mater Toilet Club, at 31 Trinity Street, (close to Pimbo's employer, Adamson the tailor) that Pimbo stared aghast at the display of new type hair-cream, far removed from his 2^d tin of Brilliantine Jelly. It was priced at 2/6 per bottle, and Mr Asbury was undoubtedly pleased with its name on the bottle – Almosa.

After a few money 'tips' from Adamson's undergraduate customers, Pimbo was able to purchase a bottle. But somehow, it didn't quite plaster his hair down to rival that of Clive Brook. Even so, the Alma Mater set a new trend in hairdressing around that part of the Town.

When Pimbo told Jenny of the opening of the Alma Mater, she gave a quick smile. "Reminds me about mum. One day, being a bit hard up, she decided to have a go at cutting my hair. I was only about six years old, and my hair was like a boy's, a sort of bob with a fringe across the eyes, so mum though a basin cut might do the job"

Noticing Pimbo laughing, Jenny broke in "Yes, you've guessed it, mum made a mess of it. So she sent me down to Scotty's on East Road with 2^d, hoping he would repair the damage. Bless his heart, he gave me the 2^d back and told me to tell mum not to try it again!"

Many boys at East Road School came to school sporting a basin-cut. You couldn't mistake it. The worst thing was, that parents didn't realise how a kid felt. Pimbo used to dread going to school after a such-like cut; he was glad to start a paper-round in order to be able to pay for a real hair-cut.

In King Street, Pimbo remembered a little barber-shop half-way down from the Common end. He couldn't think of its name, so decided not to include the barber in his research list. In any case the little shop had long since changed hands, and at the moment was run by a Mr Lanham. But Pimbo had a recollection of the former barber being a very small man, so much so, that he found it difficult to reach the top of his customers' heads. At that period, Pimbo's mother was friendly, through the Salvation Army, with a little crippled woman who lived almost next door to the barber in question. Norman's drapery shop was close by. Sometimes, Pimbo would go along with his mother as she would wash and toilet the invalid old lady. The little top room type flat, was a very poor place for such an invalid, and as far as Pimbo could remember, it was always difficult to obtain hot water. Although the premises had no bathroom, it was vital that the lady had a kind of bed-bath. It was then that the kindness of the little barber came to the rescue. He would carry up the stairs enough hot water to last out for the toiletry tasks. Sometimes, during the more intimate parts of the washing procedures, Pimbo would go down to the little shop and listen in to the old men's gossip

At about that period, a murder-case was on the tip of everyone's tongue. Many and varied were the tales Pimbo listened to; at times the little barber would look guiltily at the boy and say "Well, you've got to hear about these goings-on, you might as well hear it now – if they go too far for your age, I'll put a brake on 'em!"

Apparently, the murderer in question, was a certain Clan Waring, or some such name the murder took place in King Street. Coupled with the juicy tales was one of a certain doctor in Bridge Street, who had abused his position and committed an indiscretion warranting his being struck off the Register for a specific time.

Pimbo reckoned that the barber was such a kindly little man, who went out of his way to help others, but found the stirring yarns of his customers made up for his sometimes mundane existence, thus balancing his outlook on life. Wasn't there always a new customer who might not have heard the latest horror story?

A short distance away from the little barber, was the hairdressing establishment of R. Jones, at 50 King Street.

Pimbo was telling Jenny about how, in lessons at school, he'd heard about J.M.W. Turner, the famous painter, whose father was a barber in a humble little shop in Maiden Lane near Covent Garden. At the age of five, he accompanied his father to a customer's house where the barber serviced the weathly patron, a certain Mr Tomlinson. On his return home, the young Turner sat down and drew from memory a heraldic lion which had attracted his attention at the house.

The father, anxious that the boy would not have to 'scrape' a living in like manner to himself, decided there and then that his son would become a famous painter. Before he was thirteen the boy was sent to study under Thomas Malton in Long Acre. But Malton could not teach him elementary lines of geometrical drawing, so took him back to Maiden Lane in sheer desperation, almost shouting at the boy's father. "Mr Turner, the boy will never do anything, he is fit only to be a barber, never a perspective artist!"

The barber was far from finished with aspirations for his son. Having been left a small legacy, he put him with Hardwick, an architectural draughtsman, from where at the age of fourteen, the young Turner was sent as a student to the Royal Academy.

After leaving the Royal Academy he began teaching water-colour drawing at schools, first at five shillings a lesson, later at ten shillings, then at a guinea. He was employed to make drawings for publishers, and made views for the Oxford Almanac, thus acquiring a reputation which caused his drawings to be sort after and procuring him introductions to noblemen and dignitaries.

Mr Tomlinson, at whose house he first learnt to draw at the age of five, bought many of his later pictures, and was instrumental in introducing him to the great painter, Reynolds, who allowed Turner to copy pictures in his studio.

The words of the irate Malton had to be eaten because Turner, in after years, became Professor of Perspective at the Royal Academy. Turner, was a very shy man, who, used to cover up his drawings should anyone attempt to look at them. He painted with his door locked and only one or two of his most intimate friends ever saw him at work.

In 1812, he moved from Harley Street to Twickenham, where he was joined by his father who, had closed up his barber-shop between 1795 and 1800.

It was said that the old barber became his son's willing slave he strained and varnished his son's pictures when finished. At his death, Turner was deeply moved, he loved his father and never seemed the same after his death. As a small recognition of his dad's stay with him, Turner would say "he started and finished all my work."

Turner felt that he owed a lot to the old barber, in teaching him to scrimp and save in order to purchase his painting equipment. He would say "Dad never earned a lot during his barber-shop days, and he would never praise me for anything, *except* saving a halfpenny!"

Jenny sighed as Pimbo finished his saga on the wonderful painter. She had written quite a lot down but, seemed perplexed. "What's this to do with Cambridge barbers? People won't want to read about those days – I thought –"

"Look Jenny, you're right, but since this barber lark project started I've dug deep for extra information. You see, even a hundred years ago, barbers were held in good esteem. Turner's dad used to go out to homes and cut hair. My teacher told me that in London, some of the super-duper shops actually sell sketches and paintings. They hang them on the walls in their salons – so you see, it might even happen in Cambridge!"

"Well, if he was so good, why haven't you mentioned any of his paintings?" queried Jenny

Pimbo wasn't to be outdone and consulting his old text-book he rattled off: 'Morning on the Coniston Fells, Cumberland; 'The Battle of the Nile'; 'Shipwreck' and his masterpiece 'Ulysses Deriding Polythermus'.

"Phew!" gasped Jenny.

Pimbo laughed "Sometimes his paintings, his later works, were scorned, and ridiculed – but he was buried in St. Paul's Cathedral – not bad for the son of a common barber!"

Jenny had had enough. Pimbo at times seemed like a butterfly, flitting from one plant to another. She marvelled at his acceptance of the gang's breaking up. He rarely mentioned the other boys, who must have felt dismayed at the out-come of their once almost feverish excitement at the Time capsule plan, with a likelihood of their being accepted as something special by a neighbourhood that regarded them as mere nuisances.

Pimbo seemed to realise her silent misgivings. Touching her shoulder, he kissed her gently on the cheek. "Oh, I know what you're thinking, what sort of husband I might make if I continue my goings-on. Don't worry, Jenny, the teachers say that boys go through stages like this, they're different from girls. It's a kind of growing up – like you wanting that special blouse in Paulines. You see, I don't really worry about what I wear, as long as it's clean and tidy!"

As they walked slowly back home across Parker's Piece, Pimbo was laughing again. "Just one more barber's story Jenny. The barber who cuts dad's hair in Histon has left his wife and home and absconded with the girl who worked in his shop. She was much younger than he – I'd never do that to you, 'cut' you dead, or give you the 'brush-off!'

Jenny smiled back. She didn't like the joke, but, she loved her Pimbo.

CHAPTER 6

More Barber Tales

In fairness to Jenny, Pimbo thought it a good idea for his girl-friend to try her hand at a little research, by getting him a list of lady hairdressers. The men's world of sport and chit-chat in the barber-shop, so far had taken on a monopoly of the hairdressing trade, but the very name, thought Pimbo, conjured up a different type of skill, than the burly labourers "a bit off the top, Albert!" or "short back and sides". Then, too, he wondered what sort of chatter went on in the ladies' salons.

Jenny lost no time in procuring a list of lady 'barbers' who plied their trade in the 1926–1927 era. It ran thus: Miss A. Hardy, 19 Kimberly Road. Mrs Hodgson, 1 Parsons Court. Miss Jennings, 33 Hills Road. Miss Oldham, 57 Regent Street. Papworth L.S.C.O., 35 Regent Street. Miss Smith R.C., 57 Hills Road.

On perusing the list, Pimbo noticed that a fair percentage of the hairdressers were labelled

'Miss'. "Perhaps its just a trade name" put in Jenny "you know, like the actress. They always call themselves 'Miss', like say, Miss Evelyn Laye or Miss Sybil Thorndike!"

Pimbo, smiling of Jenny's ready wit, was pleased with her research effort, and she promised that her next venture would be that of finding out a little more concerning the clientele of the various salons. Jenny kept her promise. In a few days she came up with the following: a dear lady, whose daughter was attending the Hairdressers Foundation Guild which gave out diplomas for lady hairdressers, pointed out the reason for the suddent surge towards female hairdressers. The films were mainly responsible, the various styles displayed by such stars as Pola Negri, Nazimova, Kay Francis, Laura-la-Plante and Mae Busch with the shingle bobs, fully swepts, the fringes and, above all, the dyed platinum-blondes of Jean Harlow and her likes.

Then too, the radio commercials imploring young girls to use Friday-night as Amami night, a forbear, no doubt, of the young ladies "I can't come out, I'm shampooing my hair!" to their love-lorn swains.

The ladies' salons scored over their counter-parts, the men's, by the little extras provided. Cups of tea or coffee were a must, plus a good supply of quality magazines as opposed to the wilting dog-eared efforts in the male salons. It's possible they may have lost out in the gossip line, as, sitting motionless with a metal contraption over their heads, was not inducive to gossiping about 'her next door.'

One high-class salon, that of Mr Day of Glisson Road, whose shop was actually in Hills Road, had a very large clientele and during milk rationing found it difficult to keep up the supply of tea and coffee, but somehow, the ingenuity of the master-hairdresser got him through the crisis. As the dear lady pointed out to Jenny, most forms of hairdressing were really of a theraputic value; after a terrible war, the young people fought against dullness and mundanity, they brought out their feelings by changing hair-styles and adopting different cuts. They scrimped and saved to manage to bring out their girlhood dreams of emulating Gloria Swansons and Janet Gaynor.

Those well off enough to actually learn the trade took themselves off to various teaching establishments which, no doubt, was the reason that over the top of their shops were so many 'Miss, so-and-so, Hairstylist'.

On reading Jenny's little thesis, Pimbo realised how barber-shops actually felt the pulse of the public; how, behind the array of various toileteries displayed in the window, was a little room almost akin to the psychiatrists couch. Mr Rollinson, W. of 175–177 Newmarket Road, once told Pimbo of the heartaches he experienced during the First World War and of how young soldiers, training at Bury St Edmunds before being sent over-seas would pop into his shop for a shave or haircut. On each leave he got used to their ways and looked forward to seeing them. Gradually, with the war in real earnest, the leave periods got fewer and he lost track of their anxious young faces. Some still came in, but at the end of the war, at the final count, "I wonder what happened to young Smith? his query was met with the accustomary blank look and shrug of the shoulders.

The old barber still had a few cards sent him by his war-time customers from 'over-there', amazingly, ironically, of those who sent him cards, very few boys returned to sample his "Your next Sir!"

Mr Rollinson, was a diminutive, white haired man, with moustache to match, whose shop had been going long before Pimbo's move to Leake Street. It was through the kindly barber that Pimbo learned about the origin of the barber's pole and the reason for the red-white and sometimes blue colours. Mr Rollinson, as well as functioning as a barber, also officiated as a dentist, albeit not qualified as such, but of the 'any old port in a storm' variety which, of course was a great boon to his tormented customers.

The barber's son, weighed in at something between 18–20 stone, and was used to sit on or 'restrain' customers during the tooth pulling sessions. His loyal wife would hold back the poor man's head, and with a pair of pliers, Mr Rollinson would complete the operation. The charge would be 6^d a tooth. Boys of the Barnwell area would look in awe at the display of pulled teeth in the barber's window which, after a particularly busy period of dentistry some of great proportion, were no doubt, a good recommendation for Mr Rollinson's artistry.

The red of the barber's pole would signify either blood letting, tooth pulling, or a slip of the razor.

The white, no doubt, implied a bandage, or the pallor of the patients face during the teeth extraction and, the rarely used blue, as either patriotism, or a symbol of the blue blood of the most elite of customer; the whole thing symbolising the barber's all round ability. The poor old barbers, at the cessation of hostilities, were sometimes plagued with visits from the weights and measures inspectors.

Some, anxious to make up for lost time amidst the influx of young men 'coming back' from the war, worked fairly long hours. As Albert Scott told Pimbo; one evening the W&M inspector caught him working at 8 pm. The man was very rude and at one stage Albert felt like 'clipping' him, but not with his barbering implement.

The outcome was that Albert appeared in Court, alongside other hairdressers, and was fined 30/-. True to red-tape blunders, two weeks later Albert received notification of a new rule, that he would be able to remain open until 8pm – he never received his 30/- back!

At this time, a real stringent weights-and-measures compaign went on. A hardware shop in Mill Road was fined for measuring a portion of wire-netting with a tape-measure (cloth) instead of a metal one. Rife, too, at that time was the coming of the 'Tiger Hunt'. These men, straight from the Army, anxious to earn a living, armed with a large bodkin needle and balls of coconut matting twine, would go round homes offering to repair the edges of the then popular coconut mats which adorned most hallways and doorways, and was even used as matting inside the home.

Mr Rollinson, was lucky not to have received a visit from a W & M inspector, but maybe watching tooth extraction wasn't the Inspector's cup of tea!

Later Mr Rollinson, unwittingly, was able to turn the tables on yet another Inspector, this time it was the Health Official. The good man, seemed quite unaware of the barber's side line in tooth extraction, despite the display of magnificent molars in the window.

"You got a first-aid box?" he asked crustily. It says much for Mr Rollinson's confidence concerning dentistry, that even with the sometimes copious flow of blood during and after the extractions, the erstwhile, barber had to confess, that apart from a few cotton bandages – he had no first-aid box!

"Well, get one!" came the reply "I'll be round in a day or two. No box, and you're for the high jump!" Mr Rollingson was taken aback with the surliness of the man. It seemed that England wasn't satisfied at winning a war – it had to carry on the aggression with the very people that helped to win it.

The Health Inspector kept to his word, true to his nature he came into the shop the very next day.

"Well, what about it I can't see a first-aid box around – don't tell me it's in the post!" he rapped out.

"I'm afraid a minority of my clients, especially the fair-ground diddi coys, would think nothing of pinching a first-aid kit. They have a few accidents on the fairground – you know. But I don't want to disappoint you, my lather boy had it out earlier –

it's in the cupboard."

Turning to his lather boy, the barber told him to show the Health Official where, in the cupboard, he'd placed it.

"It should be on display in the shop, at all times!" rapped out the unsavoury man.

As though suspecting a trick, the Inspector dashed across to the cupboard before the astounded apprentice could reach there – and yanked open the door. Then it all happened!

The box, a large heavy object, had been placed very unbalanced at the top of a shelf loaded with toilet bottles, the box was really just resting against the door. The sudden wild jerk at the door sent the heavy box, and a quantity of hair-cream bottles crashing down on the hapless official.

It took ten minutes, or so, before the man regained his full equilibrium. A smiling Mr Rollinson, apologising with tongue in cheek, gently dabbed the open wound with a mixture of Savlon and water, finishing off with a well applied plaster.

"There you are then! The first customer to use my first-aid kit, I'll find a nice place for the box to be sited – my boy must in future be more careful – they just don't allow themselves time to do anything!"

That evening Pimbo and Jenny went over the material they had gathered so far. Jenny, now and again, would voice her opinion as to whether or not her boyfriend would be able to make a book out of it. Was it all a waste of time? She consoled herself with the fact that had Pimbo not been doing it – he would surely be up to something else, so she settled for what she thought was the lesser of the two evils.

As though reading her thoughts, Pimbo put matters right. "It's in years to come when our work will be more appreciated. Look at the places being pulled down, they say Burleigh-back-lane, will be the next to go, all the barbers we write about now will be historical legends. They've got safety-razors coming out now, the day of the cut-throat will be over.

Barbers, soon won't take on shaving. Hair-dressing, will have to go upmarket!" he paused to let his words sink in. "Where will Doris Hopkins get her snuff from? No 2^d sniffs will be available in years to come. Mr Cartwright who supplies these ladies and gentlemen with such luxuries will be long since gone!"

Jenny was laughing "It's taking kids like us to fathom out that people around today, will become historical facts – why don't the big-wigs cotton on, Pimbo. What's special about us?"

"I reckon we're one off kids. Instead of, like say the Bisto kids who sniff out the lovely smell of roast beef and gravy, we sniff out human stories, similar thing really. In any case, when the big-wigs speak of Cambridge, they mean colleges, dons, and Senate House degree dolloping. They don't see us in the mean little streets – I suppose we're as bad really, we don't go a bundle on any of them!"

Two days later, Jenny was full of excitement as she proudly unfolded her newly found scoop on Mr Cartwright that master-barber of Fitzroy Street.

He was born in 1868 and at the age of 20 years opened up the establishment at 25–26 Fitzroy Street owing to numbers changing, it finished up at 74–76. Cartwright's correct christian name was that of John, but he often was called Jack. Working for him for 25 years was a character Bill Smith, who lived in New Street. Bill was blessed with a club foot, which, of course, was a great handicap to him, as it often caused him a good deal of trouble, At one time it turned gangrenous which caused it to be amputated. As though this was not enough, lumps appeared on his leg, which ultimately brought about a complete amputation of part of his leg, whereby poor Bill finished up with a fitted stump.

Mr Cartwright held a barbering contract with Old Addenbrookes Hospital in Trumpington Street. Many of the great man's apprentices learned their trade during the various pre-operative shaves they carried out at the hospital. Despite Bill Smith's sad occurrence with his leg, on leaving his master's employ, it was arranged that Bill would finish his days as the resident barber of Addenbrookes Old Hospital – Bill carried on until his death – an epitaph to John Cartwright's teachings and heart.

In those days, barbers had a terrific licence to carry out almost anything they so wished; such was the faith placed on them by government officials. Removing corns and carbuncles, and in John Cartwright's case, he actually manufactured his own hair cream and lotions. On a large copper over the gas, John would stir happily away with the help of his son Sidney; and who knows what concoction came eventually on to the shelves. The elixirs of life, maybe, just as in the American films showing the travelling medicine men with their 1/- bottles of life-giving lotions and cures for every ailment – they too, pulled teeth, and extracted corns and carbuncles! John also supplied at his shop hot baths for 6^d. An innovation carried on during the wars.

Of Mr Cartwright's third marriage, eight children were born, four boys and four girls. One of the boys died at the tender age of 3–4 years, his name was Denis. Of the other boys, Sidney, who is now an Electrical Engineer, worked in his dad's shop for 13 years as did his brother Mark. Eric, a half-brother, barbered all his life, taking over a shop in 2 Corn Exchange Street, prior to Reg Pilbeam.

Incidentally, John Cartwright was 60 years of age when he took on his third marriage. His young wife of 20 years met him through her apprenticeship at the shop in Fitzroy Street.

Of the four daughters, one lived in Meadowlands, another, taking her chances in Australia where she and her husband built their own house, came to a tragic end at an unmanned railcrossing. Their car was crushed by an oncoming train, killing them both.

John Cartwright was a great-hearted man. He was Founder President of the Cambridge Albion Angling Society formed in 1905 – this office he held until his death.

In 1905, at the annual fishing contest for children, he was responsible for the transportation of 1,000 kiddies from all over Cambridge to the St

Ives fishing venue.

The Daily Mirror covered the story from start to finish. They actually visited the various groups where they fished and many pictures appeared in their subsequent issues.

Sidney Cartwright, is a member of MENSA, with an intelligence quotient of 160. He followed in his dad's wake for 13 years, then, with the intervention of war, gave up the barber's brush to take on the dynamo brush. He tells of the day he visited a certain pub at the age of 17 years. To his surprise he found his dad there, enjoying a pint.

Fearing an admonishment, he was about to slide out when his dad shouted over the heads of the patrons "what'll you have, son?" For the first time in his life, he drank a pint of mild in his father's company.

Pimbo, naturally, was very pleased with Jenny's effort. She had topped up a lot of the information he'd already gained. It was nice to get the facts from the horse's mouth. "It must be your girlish charm!" Pimbo kidded her as they both sat down to clarify and put in some kind of order their new discoveries.

Jenny wasn't having any "I'm just as excited as you now you've let me do things myself. As well as put it all down, I feel a bigger share in the project has come my way. I sense, too, how the people who relate things to me feel proud that their kin are being thought well of they dig as deep as they can for little snippets of gossip, which can never be the same as in rigid journalism!

Pimbo was smiling. When Jenny let rip, she certainly let rip, lovely words she used. Sometimes he wondered where they all came from but on the other hand, Jenny always had a book in her hand.

Just then, a good deal of shouting was taking place. Some boys, who Pimbo recognised as coming from Smart's Row, were shouting at 'Slipper' a character that always wore white plimsoles throughout summer and winter and who always was in dire need of a hair cut.

"Get you haircut, Slipper!" they bawled out.

Jenny smiled across at Pimbo, haircuts were certainly all the rage these days!

F. Mathews. View of shop front in Fitzroy Street, Cambridge.

CHAPTER 7

Albert Scott – Master Craftsman

Pimbo's next visit to Albert Scott, the master barber of 169 East Road, brought forth more revelations. At the age of 16 years Albert's dad at 120–121 East Road, in answer to an enticing ad 'Good razor men required' took himself off to Peterborough with a view to learning the trade, and thus setting himself up as a master-hairdresser. In those days, to leave home was almost unheard of, it spoke volumes for the lad's determination to get his own business.

As Albert junior was saying. There was a great deal of shaving in those days. At weekends the queue would start as early as 7 am and continue well into teatime. He reckoned that wielding a razor was in itself a gift, you either had it or you didn't. Many blooming apprenticeships were nipped in the bud because of the lad's lack of dexterity with the formidable cut-throat.

At that period, haircutting technique went no further then scissors and comb. So Albert's dad,

A. Scott's establishment. 169 East Road.

thrilled to his boots at the sign over the Peterborough shop 'Haircutting in this salon is now
done by machinery!' – the hand-clippers had
arrived!'

Albert was all smiles as he told Pimbo about the
Umbrella-man. This worthy gentleman made his
living by repairing gamps, and complete with his
array of handles and ribs, once a month, he would
call in for a hair cut. The Umbrella-man wore his
hair in a kind of 'bun', similar to that of Head
mistresses, music-teachers or frumpish spinsters.
Scott senior, would unravel the bun, let it down to
the nape of the neck, and then trim and cut the
resulting mass of hair.

On this particular day, Albert's dad had over-
done the cutting to such an extent that when it
came to re-doing the 'bun' to its former glory –
there wasn't enough hair remaining to finish the
job. The Umbrella-man exploded into a tirade of
abuse which, had it been a gale force wind, his
umbrellas would have doubled the airbourness of
Mary Poppins.

Pimbo questioned the younger Scott on the
amount of money his dad might have made in
those earlier days of the pre-war period, the 1st
World War, that is!

Apparently, his dad kept a diary in which was
entered for a certain afternoon's work, 'Not a bad
day. Total 2/9^d'. Of course with shaving at its
minimum of 1½^d and haircuts at 3^d with 6
haircuts at 3^d each, an appreciable amount of
shaves would have to be made to make up the 2/9.
Ten shaves plus the six hair cuts would be 16
customers needed to make the 2/9^d. Should these

clients all be in the shop at one sitting, the time factor would be quite great. Allowing for intervals between, the servicing, a whole afternoon's work, 2/9, was not very productive, even for those days.

As Albert pointed out, barbers had to work very hard to make a living, often delving far into the evening hours.

Jenny had just been to see Clara Bow in her latest picture 'The It Girl'. She was all agog about the star's hair-do and explaining to Pimbo was difficult. The current rage for men and boys was the Boston-cut and Pimbo saw very little else in regard to fashion, especially about 'girls', as he would put it.

Jenny had managed to steer him to the outside still pictures of Clara's film, which was showing at the Playhouse in Mill Road. As they stood on the pavement, Jenny pointed her finger at the star's beautifully groomed hairstyle. "Wouldn't you like to see me like that, Pimbo?"

"It would cost too much" he replied bluntly "Why not got to the modelling school, I think it's somewhere up Castle Hill. They don't charge you, but, you have to place yourself under the dubious craft of the apprentices."

Jenny wasn't having any! She'd heard a few tales of such-like establishments, some no doubt, a bit far fetched – but she had read letters in the Cambridge Evening News concerning irate mothers and their disappointed daughters.

Next day, Pimbo was back on the research trail. The barber was Mr Smith whose shop was on the corner of Cheddars Lane, Newmarket Road, around the 1916–1917 era. Smithy, as he was usually called, was an ardent member of the Hairdresser's Federation. He was a small lithe man, but in his latter years though he was suffering from a terminal illness. Eventually, this drove him to suicide. Whilst his wife was making him a cup of coffee, Smithy ended it all by two expert incisions on either side of his jugular vein. This brings out the fact that most barber's had an expert knowledge of anatomy at the time. It was said that the poor barber had 'done a very neat job indeed'. Running to most barber's 'true form', Smithy, took bets for both himself and the bookmakers.

Still on Newmarket Road, Pimbo came up with the amazing saga of the Mathews brothers; of five brothers, four were hairdressers of the highest order, with shops spread evenly around the Barnwell area. Herbie Mathews, was the first brother to be researched by Pimbo.

Herbert was a very small man, only about 5ft tall. His shop was listed as being next to the Bun Shop, but an easier geographical reference would be 'close to Jim Lee's well known pedlar's paradise'. Jim's shop went well back into the River Lane bowels; he sold just about everything. Pimbo could remember buying what was then called a magic lantern. It was 3^d, and extra for the penny slides; with a sheet against the wall, kids could imagine themselves at the pictures. Passing pedlars who were rife in those days, were mostly ex-servicemen far from satisfied with the adage "England fit for heroes to come home to". From Jim's place they could buy shoe-laces, matches or other knick-knacks to place on their trays, all at a wholesale price. But Jim also catered for resident citizens as well as the pedlars, selling everything from pots to watches, rings and all household goods.

Getting back to Herbie, with Jim close by, many of the passing pedlars would call in Herbie's for a quick trim or shave, in accordance with how busy they had been among the Town toffs! The pedlar's of course, were a mixed bunch, at times a little frightening to a man of Herbie's small stature. This may well have accounted for the barber's habit of continually jumping up to look out of his window, much to the annoyance of his customers.

It might have affected his wife's strange behaviour when cooking a pudding for him, she liberally laced it with carbolic-soap. Herbie, too, did a side line of taking racing bets, as did most barbers of the day.

The next Mathews brother takes us to C.F. Mathews of 5 Victoria Road. This barber had a reputation for love of the "bottle", but this in no way impaired the confidence in him shared by other barbers in the Town, because he was their recognized relief barber when they were either ill or taking a holiday! Rumours can be nasty, as some said that many barbers would have preferred to have stayed closed than risk offending their customers.

Close to C. F.'s shop was that of Taffy Gray's, who was the first man to introduce the sarsaparilla drink to small boys, Pimbo, being one such.

In the centre of his shop, was a pump-like contraption into which Taffy fed fizzy mineral gas, coupled with the sarsaparilla ingredient. With a few hurried pumps, gurgles, and hissing noises, out came the lovely dark brown drink at ½ᵈ a glass. It often broke down, with Taffy having to pay back the boys' prepaid halfpences.

Mr Mathews was also well known as the official barber for a certain 'wheel of fortune' man, whose name was derived from the wheel-barrow type of contraption which held a wheel on which was placed a kind of rub-stone that sharpened scissors and knives. This gentleman roamed the streets and byeways with his plaintive cry 'scissors to grind, scissors to grind'. C.F. would give a free haircut to the old grinder in return for his scissors to be sharpened.

The fourth barbering Mathews, was Alfred of 152 Mill Road. Alf was in residence there for many years and could be rightly described as the railwayman's barber. In those days, the early morning pavements would be pounded by the hundreds of railway-workers living in the little side streets of Mill Road, complete with their tin lunch-boxes and immaculate turn-out with spotless overalls and shiny boots. They had a very strong Union which gave Romsey Town the misnomer of Red Russia, but the men were devoted workers and took great pride in keeping the rolling stock going. Unions to them were a form of security amidst rife unemployment. Alfred Mathews did a good job by helping to make them well groomed.

In the meantime, Jenny, not to be outdone gave Pimbo a little extra low down on a barber already mentioned, Deafy Webb, who once officiated in a shop next to the 'Bird in Hand' on Newmarket

Road. Jenny pointed out that Deafy was appointed contract barber for Chesterton Hospital. It seemed that this barber was either not deft enough with a razor or used a badly honed one, because rumour had it that some patients were deliberately absent on the day of his calling on their particular ward. 'Snatching' as they called it, was an unpleasant and painful experience!

Dales Brewery too, now close at hand to Deafy was a good substitute for his regular 'pint-in-hand' from the 'Bird-in-hand' days!

Pimbo's research went on relentlessly. Next, was another Mathews brother. F. Mathews of 16 Fitzroy Street. Fred, or Frank, was there during the 1914 war, and no doubt cut and shaved a good many sacrificial lambs for the oncoming slaughter. He was present too, when the new Austin Seven Ruby saloon car was on show at New Square, where only three models displayed the larger wheels fitted as an experiment – they were not significantly a great success. Mr Mathews was a good steady workman, without supplying us with many anecdotes!

To round off the Mathews family, we have Mathews J. of 187 East Road, another excellent craftsman but one not given to many personality traits as Jenny would say! Both brothers were working as barbers in the 1914 era.

In the middle of the week, Jenny's enthusiam for barber-shop research was enhanced by her visit, with Pimbo, to the Kinema, A Charlie Chaplin comedy had our hero as a barber, going through all the rituals practised by the barbers the two youngsters had come across in their research.

The shop was crowded with burly men awaiting shaving. Charlie filled their faces and mouths with frizzy white foam. Then to the tune of the 'Barber of Seville' he proceeded to strop the cut-throat razors. With the blade, apparently superior to that of Deafy Webb's, Charlie, still in tune with the operatic aria, then shaved his hapless customer.

It brought fully to light how barbers were held in such esteem by the public. Their intimacy with customers, which few trades boasted of; the absolute trust patrons placed in men, who were armed with such an awesome weapon as a cut-throat razor, its very name instilled fear into the bravest of hearts.

Then, when it was all over, the smile, the brushing down, the handing over of the white napkin for the customer to service himself. To finish with "Was there anything else, Sir?" Charlie brought it all out beautifully. In fact, Jenny at one stage wished she produced enough bristles on her chin to merit trying a shave! The new commodity 'Veet' would have to satisfy her, when it came to shaving her legs.

"Of course, a few barbers' jokes often do the rounds at school!" broke in Pimbo "here's one that might fit our friend Deafy Webb":

Barber. "Have you been here before?"
Customer. "Yes."
Barber. "I don't remember your face."
Customer. "No – it's all healed up now!"

"Here's another one" laughed Pimbo.

A keen John Gilbert fan went to the barbers

and asked for a John Gilbert hair style. The barber, to the man's surprise wielded his scissors in a most alarming way, taking off most of his customer's hair, leaving just a little around the sides. "Are you sure you know John Gilbert's hair-style?" raved the irate customer.

"Of course I do!" said the indignant barber "I watch all John Gilbert's 'Sgt Bilko' films"

"Here' some more" said Pimbo.

Mean man. "How much for a haircut?"
Barber. "Three pence."
Mean man. "How much for a shave?"
Barber. "$1\frac{1}{2}^d$"
Mean man. "Right – shave my head."

Barber. "How do you want you hair cut, Sonny?"
Small boy. "Like Daddy's – with a hole in the top."

Bald customer to barber. "Is you hair restorer any good?"
Barber. "Any good? We had one customer who pulled the cork out with his teeth – next day, he had a handle-bar moustache!"

Jenny suddenly became earnest. Inwardly she wandered how the barbers' project was really going. Pimbo of course, in his usual vein, saw very few snags. Jenny had tabulated all the data on barbers, which so far they had collected. It amounted to a fair amount but would it be enough to write a book on? It would all have to be threaded together; as good as Pimbo was reckoned to be on compositions at school, would he be able to correlate it in sequence. There was only one thing to do – they must have a talk with Curly Northfield. After all, it was he who had suggested the project, maybe he would give them a little sounding on their progress so far – Pimbo agreed!

Curly was his usual amicable self. He was all for their carrying on. After perusing their efforts, he looked up at his two, young protégés. "Now, you two have doubts because you're looking at it from its current angle. Of course people aren't going bananas about the barbers of today, they say a prophet in his own town is of very small regard, thus it is with barbers. But in fifty, sixty or seventy years' time, those self-same men will be legendary!"

Curly paused to study the impact of his words. He then surprised them by pointing out the reaction of their time capsule venture. Tom Banks' old cottage had now gone forever but Curly, taking one more final look at the dereliction, whilst probing about the chimney piece area, came across more evidence of the two men's work. A small bundle of dog-eared yellowing scraps of note paper was found well below the surface, the heat from the fire bricks had somehow preserved the writings.

The name of a person, not quite legible, was on the bottom of the notes, but the word librarian was intact. Curly remembered that a short distance away from 'The Hole' was the East Road Reading Room. The caretaker was a small bearded man who had a reputation for being well read, which, of course, in that locality was something to be admired. Curly told Pimbo and Jenny that after all, it could have been the library-man who had helped Tom Banks and Wally in their research work.

"What are the new findings?" asked an excited Pimbo.

Curly smiled. "This in no way hinders your present project. In fact, if anything it strengthens our conviction that in time, people will appreciate what we're trying to do. I've taken all the notes found to the Cambridge Library which has passed them on to the Historical Section where they will be dealt with. There's a hint that we might get some kind of reward!"

Curly, noticing the young couple's desire to get on with it, read out the new findings. A list of books, which must have been on sale many years ago:

The Silver Library
Lang's (A) A monk of Fife: A story of the days of Joan of Arc, 13 Illus. 3/6
Merriman (H.S.) Flotman: A Tale of the Indian Writing 3/6
Buckton. Comfort and Cleanliness: The servant and the mistress question. *Crown 8VO 2/-*
Willich. 'Popular Tables' for giving information for ascertaining the value of Lifehold, Leasehold, and Church Property, the Public Funds. Crown 8VO 10/6
Froudes (J.A.) The History of England, from the fall of Wolsey, to the defeat of the Spanish Armada. 12 Vols. 3/6 each
Haggard's (H.R.) She: A history of adventure. 32 illustrations 3/6

Helmholtz. Popular lectures on Scientific Subjects.
With 68 woodcuts. 2 vols. Crown 8VO 3/6 each
Doyle (A. Conan) The Refugees: A tale of the
Huguenots. 25 illustrations. 3/6

Pimbo and Jenny burst out laughing, as did
Curly at the end of the boring list.

"One thing" said Curly "for a couple of East-
roadites, you're certainly doing fine in the book
sense – your respective teachers should be proud

Side entrance to A. Coxall's salon High Street, Linton.

CHAPTER 8

The Barber of Seville

Jenny came home from school one afternoon, full of information concerning her newly found evidence that barber shops were a most honourable profession; even in Seville, hundreds of years ago. The class was doing a project on plays which had been enacted all over the world. 'The Barber of Seville' had been, to Jenny's delight, the chosen play.

She told Pimbo of Figaro's proud boasting: everyone wants me, young boys, girls, old men, doting swains; I have always plenty of money in my pocket. Widows harass me to find them a husband, as do the opposite spouse crave of my indulgence to find them a merry widow. They beseech me to write love letters and make arrangements for them to meet. My little shop is a powerhouse of love, I have wigs to transform bald men into swashbuckling romeos, and beautiful wigs for the ladies, turning them into Gainsborough beauties to capture the men's hearts.

I am a factotum for surgeons, dentists, doctors and psychologists. In my cupboard I hold lancets, keep leeches, to lower the blood pressure of lecherous old men; all tricks of the trade for a quality barber. I am the hum of this village. I feel the pulse of all inhabitants, and yet, although they crave of my out-pourings of good advice, when they enter my shop I treat them like Lords. I hot towel their heavily jowled cheeks, pomade their false hair and brush down the evidence of their wanton meanderings.

For the ladies I do likewise, arrange their hair in accordance with the beaus they desire, but I distance myself from their flirtations. They trust me implicitly, as though I'm a mere chaperon – that way, I never lose a customer, but have many temptations that beset me!

"Phew!" gasped Pimbo "you've really lifted the lid off a barber's shop!"

Pimbo was delighted at Jenny's participation in the project. 'The Barber of Seville' was certainly an epitome of the barber's role in society, a society that was fast losing the little intimate touches a society that was now distributing its working-class inhabitants to far-flung areas of the Town, from which it would have to start all over again, to discover new treasures among the barbering fraternity.

Pimbo thought at once about Harry Scott of 9 Milford Street, a brother of the illustrious character barber of East Road – doyen of all barbers! Harry was a do-gooder in every sense of the word. Where, do-gooding came from the heart, out of a Christian motivation, not that of a social climber;

of helping someone else to climb a ladder out of poverty or sudden calamity. He organised the first Benefit Concert held in the Beaconsfield Hall in Gwydir Street. Harry did a large amount of welfare work, he was a grand Christian, attending the Christian Fellowship which embraced his area.

A barber, who died under estranged circumstances, need have little fear for his widow or family. Harry Scott would see to it that the benefit-concert would help the family on to its feet until rosier outlooks took over. A collection of, say, £32 in those days would be the equivalent of £200 or more in these days of inflation.

Pimbo was smiling at a little snippet he'd heard about Alf Mathews of 152 Mill Road. When the boy proffered 4^d to Alf for service rendered the barber would give him ½^d change. Alf, too, kept a stern eye on the comics which he had to keep the boys quiet, 'Film Fun' 'Comic Cuts' 'Chips' 'Funny Wonder', otherwise they would be stuffed up their jerseys, to be swapped at school or sold for ½^d.

Then too, was Mr W.E.G. Beattie of 3 Jesus Lane, a barber at the opposite end of the social scale to that of Harry Scott. Mr Beattie was the University barber, plying his skills to the elite of the Town. Professors, dons and academic students came under his scissors and comb! It was said that he looked upon all other barbers as mere 'shavers' fit only to scrape the chins of the working-class. A side-line to his hairdressing was that of supplying binoculars and cameras to his well heeled customers at, of course a very profitable price.

A large sign, proclaiming 'Singeing' adorned his salon walls. It was reckoned that this practice brought out the moisture from the end of the hair follicles, thus helping the hair to grow more abundantly. The resultant smell was conveniently disguised under a strong pomade, usually causing an extra tanner to be put on the bill. The whole operation of singeing was considered to be the aftermath of the old-wives-tales going the rounds during that period – no real benefit was ever discovered.

Pimbo, in case he forgot any good snippets, usually wrote them down immediately. A good one concerning Mr A.H. Scott of East Road, father of young 'Albert', was going the rounds. In the closely knit area of Barnwell, taking in East Road, Occupation Road and down to the Newmarket Road bridge, deaths due to the appalling consumption were rife. A dear midwife living next door to the Workhouse 81A Mill Road was usually called out at time of death to 'lay out' the corpse.

As most families wanted their loved ones to look their best in the coffin, Mr Scott was often called out to minister the 'last rites' in the form of a shave and trim.

A certain 26 stone man, known as Harry Quitmore and living in Occupation Road, was in this case the victim.

In those days, a candle was often the only means of illumination in the tiny homes. The Veritas mantle, priced at 3^d and being very delicate indeed, meant that should a mantle 'blow' by the middle of the week, a penny for the gas was more producible than the replacement cost of a mantle.

Thus it was that our barber hero, Mr Scott, found himself preparing to shave and minister to Harry Quitmore. The room was very small, with a large bed taking up most of the room. The prevailing light was the solitary candle which had reached almost to the end of its tallow. (Harry Quitmore's wife, too, was of immense proportions, taking up a whole pavement when they sat outside in the summer). As he approached the bed, to the barber's consternation, the candle literally snuffed it. Groping in the dark, Mr Scott found his hand resting on the cold, clammy face of the corpse. At the same time, Harry's 26 stone must have been instrumental in causing the bed, somehow, or other, to tip up! The body seemed to slide away into the darkness!

By this time, Mr Scott was in a terrible sweat. Had the corpse come to life?

Picking up his barbering kit, the barber somehow managed to get out of the room, panting and white faced, he ran from the house to the sanctuary of his shop. "That's my lot, no more 'last rites' for me!" he told an excited audience in his shop next day. Even then, the customers' faces were as white as the barber's neck towel.

But, there it was! Someone had to do it – but Mr Scott's awesome tale put fear into many barbers of the day.

Not to be outdone, Jenny related to Pimbo an incident she had ferreted out in an 1869 Chronicle of Village Life.

Mr Hills, a well loved barber of Melbourn, Cambs did most of his work by commission, that is, going to his customer's house, usually cut the hair of all the family. On 11th September, 1869 he was in Barrington, at the home of a certain Cole family, doing service to one of the children's hair. A member of the family in an adjoining room spotted what she thought to be a small dog enter the house and calmly sit down near a couch in the lounge. On inspection, she found it to be a fine vixen fox. Mr Hill, on hearing her surprised shout rushed through and calmly took the fox by her brush and ears, placing her for safety in the outside hen coop, awaiting the arrival of Mr Cole.

This worthy gentleman, of a gentle nature, and well versed in fox hunting aspects, placed Miss Reynard on the grass, then let forth arousing "Tally Ho! Hallo", which made the vixen rush round the garden at a furious rate, then to escape by breaking cover through the garden fence and quickly disappearing.

As the barber, later explained to his amused customers, "Quite a hair-raising event!"

Pimbo was getting back to the old time barbers project and had researched out a resumé of the doyen of all barbers, that of Mr Albert Scott, (father of Albert Henry Scott) of 120–121 East Road.

Albert Scott took over the above premises in 1898. Formerly, it was a butcher's shop which was taken over by a barber whose name never got beyond that of "Jack", presumably because of a likely nefarious history. In those days, many barbers had slogan boards hanging outside their shops. Albert's first job was to remove this board.

It read:

> Jack the barber liveth here,
> Shaves you clean, but, won't charge dear.
> When he's finished, pay you must,
> Jack's so poor, he cannot trust.

Albert's mother set up her son in business by borrowing £1 from the Women's Institute to which she belonged. This amount purchased four chairs, one of which was an old grandfather's chair. Accordingly, this chair was turned into the actual barber's chair. The rent for the shop was then 2/6 weekly. The Institute that so kindly loaned the £1, was situated in Wellington Street.

Bill Kemp was Albert's first lather boy at the age of 12 years (part-time). Bill graduated to the status of barber and worked for the master barber for 10 years until he was asked to manage a shop in Newmarket Road. Later he moved on his own into Fitzroy Street.

Albert went merrily on building up a fine business and refurbishing his salon. The work was done by Osbourne and Garretts of London. The whole unit was in a beautiful black and silver motif, with chairs of first class leather. It was considered at the time, to be one of the finest salons in Cambridge. With the absence of Bill Kemp, owing to his new status, a man called Asbury was engaged to assist Albert Scott in the business, this was around 1939–1942, Asbury, came to an untimely end in a drowning incident in Littleport.

A major set back cropped up with the introduction of the safety razor, round about 1916. An impetus towards this innovation came about by the then popular magazine John Bull. A figure of a stout man clad in the colours of the Union Jack adorned its front page. John Bull offered a gold plated safety razor to any of its readers who purchased the paper for 3 months. Another of its gimmicks was Bullets and Nuggets, a kind of word game, bringing in money prizes.

But the razor offer set the fashion for many young men to boycott cut-throat shaves in favour of the easy cut-proof safety razor. Representatives of the barbering trade in those early days, got very short shrift from the barbers, who turned them away most emphatically, as the fear of losing their bread-and-butter shaving income to the new fang-led safety razor worried them considerably.

After a time, young men decided that money spent on shaves at the barbers, could be utilised by allowing a fortnightly haircut to take over from the hitherto monthly visit. This gradually off-set the loss of revenue and with barbers taking on hairstyling and trimming for ladies, the barber more than made up the losses. In fact, Unisex barbering was very much in vogue. Semi-shingle, Bubble-cut, and Bobs, were accomplished as far back as 1946, with Girton students foremost in their turn for the barber's chair!

Albert Scott in the early 1940s began to deteriorate in health, so much so that his son Albert Henry was granted compassionate leave from his duties as a despatch rider, in order to run the barbering business. Albert Jr had served in the 8th Army and was awaiting orders to go to France on duty there.

The Colonel of Albert's regiment had given verbal consent that he could return to Cambridge to tend his father's health, and business, until he received confirmation concerning the amount of compassionate leave he might receive.

In true Army style-something went wrong! Albert Jr one morning was confronted by two burly red-caps (military police), ordered to put on his uniform and be taken to the nearby police station. One snag was that his army boots were in for repair, so a hasty visit to the cobblers was made in order to procure them.

Despite Albert's protest and explanation, he was kept in a cell overnight awaiting deportation to the nearest glass house for desertion. Two more days were were spent 'inside' before an apology from the War Office allowed Albert to carry on at the shop. After his dad's death, Albert took over the shop in 1946.

His dad had been a wonderful character. Many times he would give a free haircut to a person he knew was genuinely up against it. He set the stage for good workmanship and he fought against the raising of prices by the more affluent barbers in the town centre. "My little East-roaders, can't afford a penny more!" he would argue, and at the time threatened to come out of the Association of which he'd pioneered the structure.

He was ever cheerful, ready witted, sympathetic to his customers' ails, yet tolerant of their weaknesses.

Pimbo had visited his shop many times, Albert, would enquire of his family's welfare, never missing out a name of his step-sister or father.

Albert Henry slowly built up the business, catering for an almost new generation of his dad's clients.

Singeing, friction to promote growth, hairstyling for ladies and gents. Many college males as well as Girton girls frequented his salon, and still do!

Customers can be amusing, Albert told Pimbo: a customer came into the shop to buy a toothbrush. "I want a very good one!" he emphasised. Albert took one from a box marked sixpence, which the customer rejected. Then one from a 1/- box was shown. Somehow the two brushes got mixed up with their boxes. After careful scrutiny the man said "I'll take this one, it's the better brush of the two!" Unwittingly, he'd chosen the six-penny brush which had found its way into the 1/- box.

As Albert pointed out, some customers will buy an item just for the snob value of its being more expensive.

The word snob brought back memories to Pimbo of a little snippet concerning a certain Sid Maltby. This worthy gentleman had a little shoe repair business in the corner of Ram's Yard. Sid was a Jack-of-all-trades, being not averse to cutting a customer's hair in an emergency. Mr Maltby also had a very keen sense of humour and loved playing practical jokes. A certain gentleman who went by the name of Cronchie, or something similar, had at times allowed Sid to practise on his hair, which, indeed, would have taken kindly to even the basics of a basin cut.

Cronchie, worked at a dairy in Abbey Street, owned by the well known Arnold family.

He was a hard working man who, living closeby the dairy would, as early as 4 am, open up the yard in readiness for the morning's milking session. His job, too, was to fetch in the cows from Midsummer Common to Abbey Street. This action caused the street to be named "Cow-pat Alley"

Mont Eley's salon at 113 Castle Street, Huntingdon Road. "Lady" could be Mrs Webb, wife of the Betterwear brush manager.

Cronchie was an honest individual, but his appearance did not help him one whit in his approach to young ladies. This is where our Sid comes in with his practical jokes. Dressing up almost in the milk-maid tradition, Sid enticed Cronchie into a bout of courting after work on the nearby Common. Sitting on the edge of one of the cow-drinks, a concrete type of large trough to supply drink for the cattle during hot spells Cronchie prepared to accept the advances of his courting maiden.

But Sid somehow managed, before things got 'out of hand' to wriggle free, a quick movement, which toppled poor old Cronchie back into the murky depths of the cow-drink.

Cronchie, however, despite all this, still managed, to open up the gates at 4 am next morning in Cow-pat Alley.

As Albert put it to Pimbo, a barber's shop is a nursery for many tales, and over the years his dear old dad must have kept many such stories to himself. Albert remembered another slogan-board, it ran:

> This barber, plies the cleanest shave,
> With haircut, too, for you to rave,
> The sleekest skin, and hair to curl,
> Ready for your favourite girl.

CHAPTER 9

The Tales Go On!

Pimbo was getting along well with further research into the barbering realm. Leslie Neal was his next interviewee. As Pimbo had known Leslie's father from his Darwin Drive and Akeman Street days, he found talking to his son most enjoyable. Tom Neal, Leslie's dad, had been a staunch supporter of the Sally Army and despite his suffering from T.B. managed to carry the flag on the windiest of days. He was a kindly little man, and as Pimbo had once suffered from tuberculosis they both felt a kind of allegiance to each other. Tom, who lived at 10 Akeman Street, eventually died from the terrible consumptive scourge of that period.

Leslie began his apprenticeship under Walter George Ambrose at the age of 14 years. Walter's shop at 35 Victoria Road, also functioned as a newsagents; Leslie would often surprise customers by practising with scissors and comb on the edge of the shop door. Rules were very strin-

gent in those days. Josh Reed, the proprietor of
the Alma Mater saloon in Trinity Street, insisted
on his men staying behind their chairs until a
customer arrived, individual's hair would be
swept up immediately, the shop floor had to be
immaculate.

Leslie had set his heart on becoming a good
barber and mastering the cut-throat razor became
one of his priorities. Arnold's the milk magnates,
had a daily round in Victoria Road and a certain
character known as Inky was their regular milk
deliverer for that area. Inky could be seen pushing
his little three-wheeled trolley, or cart, complete
with a milk churn in the centre, around Victoria
Park at the earliest of hours, ladling out the milk
into jugs left on the doorsteps.

As Inky was such a genial character, Leslie was
allowed to practice shaving on the old milkman.
One snag was, that besides having an unruly
moustache, Inky had a mole on the left side of his
face, an area which taxed the skill of the keen
young apprentice. Leslie took a long time before
he dare attempt to surmount the top of Inky's
formidable mole. Walter Ambrose would help out
until Leslie was deft enough the slide the cut-
throat over the offending hairs on Inky's mole!

In 1936, Leslie became what is known in the
barber's world as a junior gent, the other status
symbol was that of Improver. He terminated his
apprenticeship with Walter Ambrose and sought
his fortune in Southend, where he polished off any
rough edges in his work, to return to Cambridge
after a year's break and joined forces with Jimmy
Parnell of Green End Road.

Having been with Walter Ambrose for four years, Leslie stayed with Jimmy Parnell for three years. His next move was to Count Prziborsky in 9 Round Church Street. Prizzie was a great friend of the Blue Barn Cafe proprietor, next to Marshall's printing works. The friendship accounted for the hordes of students' cycles lined up outside Prizzie's salon.

Prizzie's salon catered for the most elite of customers charging, which then was a most exorbitant fee, 9^d for a haircut as opposed to the regular 6^d touch of other barbers in the Town. At that time, Joshua Taylor opened a super-deluxe salon with eight chairs, but even they charged only 8^d per haircut.

Prizzie was the first barber in Cambridge to use a special hair contraption, which guaranteed to brush into submission, the most unruly of hair. It was about 2ft long, with a switch at one end; in its centre was a kind of large type hair roller as ladies use in perms. When switched on, it really tackled the hair as competently as a rotator will rummage among the toughest of weeds. Leslie pointed out to Pimbo that he used the 'brush' with trepidation, as it had no earth wire. Prizzie was among the first barbers to introduce the hair dryer, although he had only three chairs in the salon.

Freddie Osbourne was a barber working with Leslie at Prizzie's, Leslie it seemed, had no recollection of Prizzie himself working as a hairdresser but he stayed at Prizzi's for two years, after which he joined the R.A.F. helping to see off Hitler.

In 1947, returning from the war, Leslie found

that Freddie Osbourne had taken over at 9 Round Church Street in Prizzie's apparent retirement. Although firms were supposed to take in returning ex-servicemen, Leslie was told that there was not enough work at Prizzie's to re-engage him. This came as a surprise because a great number of service personnel billeted in colleges, on courses etc, provided plenty of casual customers. However, our hero opted for a sojourn with Percy Reed, who had opened an establishment in Mill Road close by St Barnabas Road. This shop was considered ultra-modern being the first to use the fluorescent lighting and it had three chairs and four ladies' cubicles.

After two years, Percy handed over the shop to a Pamela Watson, with Leslie taking over the management of the men's section, which he did for 35 years until his retirement; while Pamela bossed over the ladies' section.

Percy Reed moved over into another deluxe establishment in King Street, later to open up another branch nearby. In the meantime Freddie Osbourne, with a new development taking over Prizzie's area, was approaching retirement age. Although living in Lovell Road, he rented a small shop in a side road off Trumpington High Street, almost opposite the Unicorn, where it was good-humouredly said that it was better to have a haircut in the early morning as dear old Freddie liked a lunch-time pint and the finished job might not be up to Freddy's usual professional standard. At times, Freddie would tell a waiting client "Buzz off" should he have just returned from his Unicorn pint.

In further talks to Leslie Neal, the good-
natured barber told Pimbo that he regretted not a
single day of his hairdressing years. He'd met so
many wonderful people, learnt so much about the
frailties of life. Barbering had never been a well
paid job. People thought that maybe, because
many men opened up on their own after apprenticeship, that the money was good – in many cases
'opening up' had been the culmination of a family
whip-round.

The work in the old days was hard; with no
hydraulic chairs, barbers had to stoop down, or
edge up on their toes, to reach the customers' hair.
It caused a good deal of muscle ache, because of
the unnatural stances they had to adopt. Shaving
in the city centre, was never a bread and butter
line as in the East Road area, and poorer districts.
The advent of the safety razor caused only the
inconvenience of lighting the 'steamer' which provided the hot towel service, only for its use to be
curtailed day by day.

Pimbo tackled Leslie about the controversial
singeing aspect, to which no one seemed to have a
real logical answer. His answer was a little technical for Pimbo: amino acids in the body deter-
mine the length to which hair will grow. That is
why some people can grow shoulder length hair
and others have to be content with hair much
shorter. When hair reaches its growing point, it
splits into tiny tails. Women sporting 'buns' and
such-like styles, found that when plaited or pin-
ned, it split hair tails which made them stick out,
giving a fuzzy or woolly appearance.

Tapers were then used to burn of this fluff. That

is how singeing originated, affecting both men and women alike. Many men wore beards and heavy moustaches at that time so singeing was considered a perk, as was shaving, shampooing and hot towels, which have followed since.

Housewives tales give us: that the thinning ends of the hair cause men to catch colds. Thus singeing would alleviate the possibility of their catching cold. As Leslie pointed out, "You pays your money and takes your pick!"

Before leaving Leslie, Pimbo received a little more info from the now retired barber.

A barber, Dodger Farren, once worked at Prziyborsky's and after leaving, opened up a shop at 20–22 Herbert Street. The front room was the salon and Dodger did a good service for a number of years, pending his retirement.

A certain barber, Charlie Gould of 39 Castle Street, gained a reputation for being the two-minute barber. 'Short-back-and-sides', apparently being his stock in trade and the 'fastest clippers in the west' (side of Cambridge).

Mont Eley, another stalwart whose shop reached almost into Huntingdon Road, kept his barber's pole going well after the majority of other peers. He seemed proud of his working symbol. It was from Mont that the following story went the rounds.

A small boy was behaving in a truculent manner whilst having his first haircut. The barber, to quieten him down asked "Do you know who God is?"

The young scamp replied "Yes, mister, it's that man what saves the Queen!"

Jenny was putting in her pennyworth by re-minding Pimbo about the young would-be-barber from Italy, a story that her mother, as a part-time nurse, had told her many times. This young man had arrived at Fulbourn Hospital with a view to settling down as a part-time barber; a job he had done in a mental Hospital in his own country. Jenny's mum had told her how Tony had been touched by the old, demented patients' reaction to having a shave. How, with their brain completely gone, they would hold their heads in a dignified manner and screw their faces in readiness to receive the cut-throat razor in awkward places on their chins. It seemed that the years were rolled away and they were back into the days when appearances were a main priority; a reflex action they would never lose.

Jenny added the final touch. Tony had been given a lift by car down to his new lodgings in Maid's Causeway. As it was during a very wet spring, Tony was sporting an immaculate Italian made raincoat. As he stepped out into the road a passing car's wing mirror caught the belt of his raincoat, ripping down one side. The momentum threw him across the bonnet of his friend's car. Without viewing the complete wrecking of the raincoat his friend gasped out, "My! Tony, you were lucky, another six inches and you could have been killed!"

The young barber just couldn't understand, why he was termed 'lucky'. "But look at my new coat – it's ruined!" he lamented. Tony was going to learn much more during his stay in England, about our ridiculous, idiomatic speech!

That evening Pimbo and Jenny went over their work so far on the Barbers of Cambridge project.

"We seem to be jumping from one to another, then back to a certain barber a second time" Jenny pointed out.

Pimbo wasn't worried. "It makes it more natural, more spontaneous. Each day, talking to different people, I pick up little snippets concerning a barber that we have written about – we must use every anecdote available. Another thing, Jenny, when this book is finished, someone will say, after they'd read it, "He didn't mention about so-and-so doing this, or that! Now they can't say we've skipped anything!"

In this respect, Pimbo's return to Albert Scott Jr, brought out another point about Prziborsky's patent hair brush-roller. A similar type of brush was also used by other barbers. A lather boy, behind a curtain in lieu of electic power, would manipulate a handle to give the brush its momentum.

Health Inspectors, in time, boycotted the brush because of its unhygienic aspects. Alopecia, a scourge in those days, was attributed to the use of this brush attracting unwelcome bacteria, so most barbers curtailed its use.

Albert went on to say how the move to his present position from that of his dad's old shop, came about. New developments were rife, the building of the Elizabeth Bridge was in the offing, consequently, a move to a fresh site was a *must*.

At that time, dear old Mr Green, the barber at the corner of Burleigh Street, was about to retire. A private house next door to his shop was also on the market. With a view to making a double-fronted concern, Albert applied to purchase this house, as well as taking over Mr Green's establishment. But the powers that be, somehow put a spanner in the works over his application, leaving Albert, still thankful, as the new proprietor at 169 East Road. The private house made way for the Winton-Smith slaughter house.

With Pimbo's prompting, Albert brought out a few more anecdotes about his time as a barber in the East Road area. The barber's shop in Histon, mentioned previously concerning the proprietor's absconding with a younger woman and leaving his small children, was taken over by a character name 'Dye', 'Dai' or 'Die'. This barber was an ardent pigeon fancier who bored his customers with his incessant chatter about his prize birds. As far as Albert knew the shop still exists.

Cambridge's oldest working barber, then went on to talk about his dad's old customers. One, a certain Jack Raiment, was a metal, rags and wool dealer. Jack was the most generous of men, who had a clock installed over the top of Kefford's cycle repair shop. Around the dial were the words 'Time Will Tell' twelve letters in harmony with the hours of the clock dial.

At Christmas, the dealer would supply boots and toys to the poor and needy. He was a regular customer of Scott Sr and when ill, Jack would have the barber service him at his home, always paying double for the work.

Jack owned quite a bit of property, taking up half the length of Nelson Street. Ironically, hard times found their way to the kindly man's door-

The famous "Time Will Tell" clock of Jack Raiment, on East Road.

step, and Jack's affluency wilted away into obscurity. 'Time will tell' on poor Jack's clock dial, but it is a two edged sword, because Time has told a tale of generosity from a lovely man!

Albert's dad, too, was a generous man. In his day, doing the rounds were a quartet of wonderful characters: Stepper, Okie and Sluice, known as the S.O.S. men, outside this trio was Bill Westley. Mr Scott Sr, gave these men a free haircut. Bill Westley was a little man with a patch over his eye. Straight out of Dicken's was Bill, a little white dog, ever at his feet. His house in Nelson Street, although one-up-one down, the 'up' was never used, Bill did everything in the bottom room.

The room was full of rags collected by Bill in his pram around the elite areas of Newton Road and Barrow Road. A well known lady, mother of a noted character, Joe Grays sometimes known as 'Chef', or, 'Sheff', would sort our Bill's rags for him, putting them into saleable items of second-hand clothing. These were grabbed at eagerly by hard-up mothers; shirts1^d, socks $\frac{1}{2}^d$ a pair trousers 6^d, coats 6^d, even shoes at 3^d or 6^d respectively and dresses 6^d.

Bill would relate to Albert's dad, whilst undergoing a shave, all his adventures during his totting rounds.

Then there, was Stepper, known as such by the immense strides he took whilst walking along the confines of the back-of-Barnwell areas. Stepper seemed to live entirely from hand-outs he would jokingly say "I never went to school – I was too poor to pay attention!"

The most lovable of all Scott Sr's 'free' customers was David Tarrant. David was born with a low IQ, consequently needing a good deal of supervision. Unkind boys would shout at him calling him rude names, one being that of 'Jug-of-water', presumably, because of David's inability to shave himself.

He was a keen follower of the Sally Army. On Sunday he could be seen marching proudly with the Sally band around the streets of Barnwell, Mr Scott always making certain that David was well groomed for the occasion. David lived in the vicinity of Cheddars Lane.

Ironically, somehow David never was fitted out with a Sally Army uniform. But on the death of his mother, with no one to supervise his needs, he went to Saffron Walden under the care of a relative. It was then that David received his uniform, a sight of which his mother would well have been proud.

David, before his departure to Saffron Walden, could often be seen manning the gate as he called it; a kind of bar to stop grazing cows from Arnold's dairy from entering Walnut Tree Avenue. Cyclists, were it not for David, would have to dismount from their cycles, perhaps making them late for work. Some would give him a ½^d or 1^d for this service, others would slip through without as much as a greeting.

But ask David "Where do you work?" he would proudly reply "On the gate, Sir, on the gate!"

Undoubtedly a barber's shop saw it all happening; because, with a towel around your neck and a cut-throat at your throat, barbers' had a way of making you talk!

Pimbo, suddenly remembered a barber from his old village Bottisham, one such, Jack Goody. Mr Goody worked from his house next door to Moppy Coleman the baker. With a line of German P.O.W's, Jack, short of time, was hurriedly snipping them off in assembly line fashion. Getting back to camp, the Sergeant found that one prisoner's hair had been cut only on one side. Jack finished him off next morning!

CHAPTER 10

Pimbo Joins the Barbers' Fishing Trip

To help out with holiday money, Pimbo took a job as lather boy with Mr Cartwright the well known barber of Fitzroy Street, as previously described. Pimbo commenced duty on Saturday morning, a time when even the working class had a little money, with time to spend it. The building opposite Mr Cartwright's shop, was used for several purposes, one being band practice for the Fifth Company Boys' Brigade. Pimbo's first customer was a man known as Slipper, on account of his everyday footwear being a pair of cheap white slippers bought from Woolworth's at six pence a throw!

At that moment the boys' band was striking up a march known as 'Knocking at the Dead Man's Door' and for a moment Pimbo found himself lathering Slipper to the time of the stirring march.

"New, ain't yuh boy?" asked Slipper, breaking

the sequence of the boy's lather brush. "Better keep plenty of lather going, I can only afford a shave once a week!"

Pimbo had heard many tales concerning Slipper. Boys told of his relentless chasing at the first call of his nickname – he would chase a boy from one end of the town to the other. It was told of a boy, having to escape his wrath entered the pictures, only to find Slipper waiting outside at the end of the programme!

The slip-slop of the cut-throat razor running over the sharpening strop, gave a hint to Pimbo to get a move on. Mr Cartwright slid skilfully over the tough bristles of his customer, who wilted only when the barber's fingers tweaked his nose in order to shave the awkward spot between lip and nose.

A spluttering and spitting out of a mouthful of soap brought Pimbo out of his day dreaming play of watching the master-barber.

"You, boy, look what you're at – call yourself a lather-boy!" Mr Cartwright won't get customers calling twice when you're around!" Slipper rounded off his tirade by jumping from his seat and vigorously wiping his smarting mouth.

Pimbo's heart sank. This would surely mean the sack! Glancing across to Mr Cartwright he was relieved to find the genial barber, giving him a sly wink. "I'll deal with him in good time. It's his first day, he'll probably get another chance." The barber's reassurance did little for Slipper's equilibrium. Paying his 2^d, the irate customer stomped out into the street.

With the shop less busy, Pimbo offered his

apologies. "Just don't do it again boy, you were too busy watching me. I can't afford to lose customers. But I was a lather boy myself once, and dropped a mugful of hot water down a customer's neck."

At the end of the day, Pimbo waited for his hard-earned money. Mr Cartwright, as soon as the regular staff had departed, called a nervous Pimbo into the small annexe at the side of the salon. He pointed at a large poster which read: 'Children's Annual Fishing Contest. Tickets from Mr Cartwright, Hon. Sec. Cambridge Angling Society'.

The master-barber, smiling at Pimbo, said. "You see, I love kiddies. A boy at heart, that's me. I always reckoned that day dreamers make good anglers. Imagination, that's what's needed by anyone taking up fishing – what about it boy, want to have a go in the Annual Contest?"

Looking across to the fine display of fishing rods sold in the annexe, Pimbo glanced up at his part-time boss. "A button, string, and bent pin, that's all I know about fishing, Sir! Besides, I couldn't afford a real fishing rod. I'm sorry, Sir."

Rustling his fingers through Pimbo's shock of red hair, Mr Cartwright smiled. "I've heard plenty about you, Pimbo. A mouthful of soap wouldn't harm Slipper, anyway. I can loan you a rod, and give you a free ticket; you can have a good day out – it'll put colour in you cheeks."

The day of the contest was fine. As they approached St. Ives, Pimbo looked back at the excited faces of the children. Eager little bodies, clutching at the various types of fishing equipment, some more experienced than others many, too, with parents a little more affluent, had proper baskets, hauling-in nets, Thermos flasks, and clothing which allowed for a wet day.

Others, Pimbo could spot the cheapest of rods, even a jam jar or two, carrying a bottle of lemonade in one tight little fist, the other clutching at the rod, which might turn out to be a magic wand to haul in the biggest fish, and thus win a prize. The snake-like throng jostled its way over the narrow bridge, banners depicting from whence they came waving at cameras, as they flashed before them, Pimbo had heard a rumour that the Daily Mirror was to record the event, and follow them through the day's proceedings.

Mr Cartwright had given Dick Chapman, a boy two years older than Pimbo, the job of seeing him through the initial stages of the contest. In a quiet stretch of water, Pimbo and Dick awaited, with rods at the alert, for a prize winning bite.

Pimbo, was musing over the fact that Dick had a reputation for being on a very short fuse concerning his temper – not the best selection for a fishing guide, thought Pimbo!

Looking down the stretch of river, Pimbo could see other children lined up at convenient distances from each other. The spires of a church could be seen in the distance, an officious looking gentleman in tweeds and carrying a clip-board was walking up and down the river bank.

"He's the adjudicator, sort of referee!" filled in Dick. "Here to see fair play miserable blighter, though, told me off last year because I was smoking a woodbine!"

To Pimbo's surprise, a small rowing boat was

splish-splashing its way towards them. It had come from the northside of the river and its occupant seemed incapable of setting a straight course.

"Hi!" shouted Dick "Keep away from here – this is a fishing contest. You're not supposed to be on this side of the river – shove of, or I'll do you!"

The adjudicator, to Pimbo dismay, was nowhere to be seen. The occupant of the boat, glared back at Dick "Who, do you think you're talking to! I'm old enough to be your father. If I want to row, I jolly well will!"

Looking along the river back, Dick spotted two large bricks used for bank emplacements. "O.K. cocky! Another yard and you'll cop one of these, It won't do you, or your boat any good."

The man, however, seemed bent on self-destruction. He continued his erratic course over the fishing area of the two contestants. Dick, bricks in hand, waited until the boat drew level then, as an athelete throws the putt, he hurled the bricks toward the man and the boat. Hardly believing the eyes, Pimbo watched the effect of his friend's drastic action.

With a loud plop the bricks landed in the bottom of the boat; came a noise similar to that of splitting wood, a gurgling sound, followed by something akin to a sudden rush of water. Frantically, the man began baling out water, but to no avail, as very soon the boat sank into the depths of the river.

Dick took one frightened look at the disaster, then scampered away in the direction of the other anglers.

Grasping the large hauling-net Mr Cartwright had lent him, Pimbo leaned out as far as he dare, waiting for the floundering unwitting bather to grasp it. Luckily, the flow of the river brought him closer to the bank, where Pimbo was able to push the net handle within reach of the hapless man. With a kind of dog's paddle, the man eventually reached the bank to safety.

By this time the adjudicator, with a panting Dick behind him, arrived on the scene. Allowing the bedraggled man time to regain his composure, the judge turned on Pimbo, "What's all this about? Were you anything to do with the boat sinking? Might as well check your competition number – not an imposter are you?"

Producing the ticket and form Mr Cartwright had given him, Pimbo nervously awaited the official's next move.

"Uh'm, seems O.K. Well, anyhow, what happened?"

Making an effort not to incriminate Dick too heavily, Pimbo gave the best account he could. At the same time, feeling that Dick had lived up to his short-fuse reputation and wondering how Mr Cartwright could have so much faith in Dick as an angler and mediator!

"You'll pay for the boat young man. I want your name and address. A chap with your temper ought to be locked up!"

Although soaked to the skin, the man managed to make his presence felt.

For the first time, the adjudicator turned his attention on to the victim of the fracas. "By the way, you should not have been rowing in the vicinity of the angling contest. There are signs to this effect along the whole area of the river, which takes in the fishing rights of the competition."

Turning sharply, the official glared at the little group. "I've got all your names, I shall look into the matter after the contest. It's my job to afford pleasure to those sensible enough to get into a position to enjoy it! Let's have no more tomfoolery – this isn't the behaviour likely to help youngsters become good anglers!"

In the lull of the silence, Dick was putting it to Pimbo "I reckon my upbringing's responsible. The Probation Officer said that I solve all my problems with violence, that's why Mr Cartwright lets me go fishing. He reckons that waiting for fish to bite might do me a power of good - patience wise. What's your problem, first time ain't it?"

"I'm his new lather boy, stuck a mouthful of soap in poor old Slipper's mouth – you know, him as always wears white plimsoles. I don't think Mr Cartwright allowed me to come for any special reason, unless to stop me worrying."

Shouts and intermittent shrieks of delight told the two boys that many of the children had managed to pull in a number of catches. For them, the churned up muddy looking water, told its own tale. A shrill note from the adjudicator's whistle caused a buzz of activity along the length of the river bank.

Youngsters were packing away their fishing gear; the judges, armed with small sets of scales, were busily weighing samples of the ample catch made by the children. Dick, a trifle shamefacedly, began helping Pimbo to pack away what was to him, rather unfamiliar equipment.

"I'm not cross with you, Dick." said Pimbo, "you were good in running for help, and it's not your fault that I've caught nothing. In fact I like you very much, I know now why Mr Cartwright allows you to come along. You're a character, Dick, just like I see in the barber's shop. Just try and count ten more often!"

Gathered together, the one thousand or more, happy fishers made their way to awaiting transport. Dick seemed to have regained his confidence. He led the youngsters in choruses of 'John Peel' 'Strawberry Fair' 'Danny Boy' and 'We are the Cambridge boys' not forgetting Jenny's favourite 'The last Rose of Summer.'

At Cambridge, Mr Cartwright was seen talking to the adjudicator, both men looked hurriedly across to Dick and Pimbo. Moving away out of the sight of the two men, Pimbo wondered what might be the outcome of the day's angling incident. He thought of the old catholic saying "Tomorrow will be Friday – and we've caught no fish today!" Perhaps he might get the sack? But somehow he knew Mr Cartwright would be fair.

As the adjudicator left, the master-barber came over to Pimbo and Dick "Stop worrying lads. The chap in the capsized boat was a crank, he's caused trouble before. He's mad because we have refused to relinquish our fishing rights on that part of the river. Belonging to a small private angling club of toffs, he expects no one but his club to fish in that particular stretch of the river."

Mr Cartwright smiled at the lads' look of relief, then went on:

"He's a bachelor, children to him are an eyesore, seeing them as anglers in his so called sacred waters, adds grit to his obsessional will – but, in future Dick, watch your temper!"

Pimbo was smiling mischievously. As they were singing their way back along the river bank, he'd remembered the Paul Robeson film "Sanders of the River". He had tried to fit the incident of the brick crashing into the bottom of the boat, and match it with the original boat song – but, the anxiety on the face of Dick, prevented words from coming.

Mr Cartwright wasn't finished. "Fishing is a grand sport, like in the barber's shop you meet all sorts." Drawing from his pocket a small red book, he read out the following:

'Rivers and the inhabitants thereof, were made for wise men to contemplate, and fools to pass by without consideration. Let me tell you, there be many that have forty times our riches, that would give the greatest part of it to be healthful and cheerful like us; who have eat and drink, and laughed and angled, and sung and slept, and rose next day, and cast away care, and sung and laughed, and fished again. And upon all that, are lovers of virtue, and be quiet, and go angling – study to be quiet!'

"From the 'Complete Angler'" smiled Mr Cartwright. "I suppose, young Pimbo, that you were suprised by my choice of Dick as a representative of all that stands for?"

The boys stared at the genial barber, awaiting his reply.

"Jesus chose Peter. He was a fisherman, but a

man of quick temper. Dick, you're no angel, but it shows that no one is perfect. Let it be a lesson to you both!"

Scott Senior's hairdressing salon, established in 1898.

CHAPTER 11

More Barber Shop Tales

As Pimbo was told, Leo North, living on East Road, a long term customer of Albert Scott, was indeed a character straight out of the old American films, where the travelling barber-cum-medicine-man-cum-conman, bemused the simple country folk into parting with their hard earned pennies.

Leo visited most of the fairs of the day, even venturing into King's Lynn. Bottles of coloured water, in lieu of cough mixture, sold at 1/- a bottle, plus the elixirs of life thrown in for a tanner. The main string to our hero's bow, however, was his 'chains' display. Here, Leo would invite an onlooker to tie him up with a length of imposing looking chain. Most, out of sheer devilment made a good job of it leaving Leo, stripped to the waist, red faced, and struggling to get out of them. Panting and writhing, Leo, to a hail of cheers from the onlookers, would finally free himself with a theatrical flourish, then pass around the hat for his crust of bread.

One day, at the May bumps, held in Fen Ditton, Leo found disaster awaiting him. Among the crowd of gaping onlookers were two sailors, home on a bit of shore leave. Undoubtedly, well versed in the tying of complex nautical knots, the two tars made a handsome job of binding Leo more firmly than usual. As Albert often related to his customers "I could see Leo turn from red-faced to that of blue. I'm sure he would have been a goner had I not rushed forward to extricate the poor chap!"

Smilingly, Albert would add "Now, everytime I hear the song 'Take these chains from my heart-and set me free' I think of Leo North."

Leo, however, had in his wife an excellent partner in the duping stakes. This lady presented herself as a fortune-teller-extraordinaire.

Her amazing props included a kind of fish tank amply filled with water. At the bottom of the tank, floated a kind of plastic doll which was attached to the side of the bottom of the tank. On the pressing of the button, the doll would surface to the top of the tank, holding a kind of waterproof envelope. Inside the envelope was the gullible customer's fortune telling gimmick. Leo and his wife were a fascinating couple, most of their work being done with tongue in cheek. Failing health which caused Leo to take longer and longer to free himself, eventually brought about his retirement. Their little house, with two stone steps leading up to the front door, and a basement cellar serving as a kitchen was of course, long since pulled down!"

Another noted customer of Albert Scott, was Mr

Wyer the chimney sweep. Formerly of Occupation Road, later to move into East Road, the sweep owned a little donkey which carried around his rods and bags of soot. Mr Wyer's reputation as a hard taskmaster to his donkey was born out by the comical sight of the sweep, stick in hand, chasing the little animal all over the Barnwell area, an incident which was a common occurrence. Mr Wyer, was however, a hard working man, small but very wiry, and seemingly always in a hurry.

His wife accompanied him on his rounds helping with the actual sweeping of the chimney, such as cleaning around the base of the hearth and chimney block. This caused the lady by the end of the day, to look a 'right sorry mess', as it was useless to wear anything the least bit glamorous.

The story goes that the poor lady, having been knocked over by a passing vehicle, lay unconscious in East Road for three hours passers by actually taking her inert form to be a bundle of old rags.

The amazing couple left Cambridge in an air of mystery. It seems that having moved into East Road, a few years later a wealthy relative left them, in a will, a completely furnished house.

The Wyer's belongings, furniture etc., was put up for sale at the lowly price of 5/-. There were no takers! The lucky couple left their house as it was, leaving Cambridge for ever. No one knows what became of the little donkey, or whether the Wyer family pursued their soot-removing vocation.

Albert had cut the sweep's hair for many years, as he did like service for his wife. They lived hard,

worked hard, and Albert would love to think that
their new house was somewhere in the country
with, maybe, a little meadow for the donkey to
graze in!

In between Albert's memory jogging, Pimbo had
researched out a barber, Mr C. Lanham of 34 King
Street. This man was an ardent believer in getting rid of hard skin. This malady made the feet
ache, and for hard working labourers at the end of
the day, to soak their feet in a bowl of warm soapy
water – was a heaven sent boon.

Mr Lanham however, always recommended Union Jack paste which came in little round boxes
complete with a picture of the flag. The boxes of
paste came fixed on a card which the barber kept
on prominent display on his shop door.

As the boxes were sold, in the vacant place left
on the card, Mr Lanham would stick pieces of
hard skin, now removed from the aching feet
brought in by relieved customers. This was a
forerunner to the chiropodist who, eventually, put
Union Jack out of business!

Another visitor most regular to Albert's salon,
was a character known as "Kingy". He was
dressed in a most bizarre fashion, in a kind of
shepherd's smock, gaiters and wearing a typical
Sherlock Holmes hat. Usually, he carried with
him a kind of shepherd's crook. Kingy it seems,
had racing in his blood, rumour having it, that,
having won a large sum of money on the horses,
the actual waiting for his winnings caused his
mind to go, hence his eccentric behaviour afterwards. Others say that the money was left him in
a will. Many and varied were the tales going

around in the barber's shop. One such, that Kingy would enter a baker's shop, grab a bread roll, then impale it on the end of his crook. Holding it aloft, he would say "Just like my horse – high bred."

Kingy lived for years on Newmarket Road in a house named 'Rocksand' – a most eccentric character, and well loved in the Barnwell area.

Mr Scott Sr, Albert's dad, showed a great interest in the Working Men's Club, an interest which his son now pursues. At that time, the Fellowship House was underway, the building being situated at the bottom end of Fitzroy Street. Pimbo, at the age of seven, entered one of their Saturday morning concerts for the kiddies, at which a prize was given for the best performance in singing, dancing, or telling a joke.

Pimbo won 7/6 for singing 'Molly Malone – in Dublin's Fair City', as he remembered later he'd missed out a complete verse. Bo Crouch, a customer of Albert's, would tell him stirring tales of the generosity of the young students that helped run the Fellowship House. They would take him round their college, give him muffins for tea, and invite him to bowl in the college nets.

Poor old Bo Crouch, the type of bowler that makes the ball break in on its fourth bounce, would shout across the street to any passer-by that he knew how he'd got the grad's in two minds on what to do with his 'leg breaks'.

Bo, always to be seen riding a cheap cycle, feet at angles with the pedals, a most cheery fellow keeping Albert in fits of laughter with his tales. Any small blessing in his life of unemployment and poverty, was accepted by Bo as a veritable windfall – a lesson to many money grabbing client of the day.

Most of the Fellowship House members were out of work men, or young boys just left school. With Albert's barber shop so nearby, most frequented his establishment. Both Albert and his dad gave many of them a free haircut. Often, some would call in on the way to the pawnshop, holding their brown paper-wrapped pledges. Sometimes the parcels were shown as security against a haircut or shave, to be paid for after a visit to 'Uncles' – a few conveniently forgot!

Almost opposite Scott's salon was the sweet shop of Charlie Reynold's. Pimbo's auntie Doris, was Charlie's sweetheart. Charlie has been a customer of the Scott family for over 60 years. Now, at the ripe old age of 80 years, Charlie now living in Sawston, making the journey to East Road for a regular haircut. Pimbo remembers his grannie chiding Charlie for having so much grease on his hair it stained the wallpaper when he leaned back in his chair.

In those days, well greased hair was the 'in thing'.

East Road, and the Scott's hairdressing business, seemed to be a magnet for a host of characters who either lived on that famous Road or in its near vicinity, many of course, being regular customers. One such, was Sonny Thurston. This young man had the misfortune in a motorcycle accident at the corner of Abbey Street, to lose a leg, the compensation from which he was able to set up a fish shop in East Road.

Nearby Albert's shop used to be the East Road

Reading Room. Fifty years after it closure, a customer walked into Albert's shop asking its whereabouts. Apparently, the caretaker of the reading room was a certain Mr Bailey who, it seems, was an ardent literary man, some of his family 'making it' to college. He kept the place immaculately clean, polishing lino to an extreme. The newspapers and magazines were locked to their lectern-type easels, a heat-giving-out tortoise stove, lured many young boys from the nearby East Road school, into the reading room to sample the welcome heat. Mr Bailey would chase them out, bemoaning the boot-prints on his beloved polished lino.

Another customer of Albert's, Hocker Hempstead, was a regular helper in the Fellowship House Club. Hocker, a name no doubt derived from his ability to kick a football with his left foot, was used by the undergraduates as their symbol of what a working class youth could do in the sporting sphere. Hocker's left foot was lethal, in inter-university matches on the college grounds, he would send the ball crashing into the back of the nets.

After a match on a local pitch, Hocker would bring several of the grads into Albert's shop, whereby a good relationship twixt Town and Gown was established. For a number of years after Hocker's death in the war, Albert continued cutting students' hair. Pimbo of course was roped in by the students who did wonders for the boys of the East Road area. Pimbo, a keen cricketer scored very well during practice matches run by the grad's on Parker's Piece. But, in the excitement of a challenge match against the student's rival college, Pimbo, managed to get out first ball. Any amount of doughnuts and ice-cream failed to comfort him. He really thought that he'd let down the whole Fellowship House policies of giving a chance to the poorer lads!"

Whilst Albert cut his hair, Pimbo would pour out his troubles but, a special Clive Brook parting usually saved the day, if not the match!

As Albert was saying, through his dad's barber shop window, he'd seen the Barnwell area go through a terrific transformation. On the corner of Occupation Road had been a kind of doss-house for vagrants. The owner did what he could for them, supplying a bath-house at the rear of the building where everyone could see them taking a bath. Then feeling fine enough to manage a trip to Scott's salon, they would submit the friendly barbers to an accent which had travelled the country. Tramps in those days were plentiful, an aftermath of the First World War. Pushing a pram holding all their worldly good, they would journey from one workhouse to another.

Pimbo remembered a tale told by an orderly at the workhouse, 81A Mill Road, how a tramp had collapsed in the street and it was found that both his legs were eaten up with ulcers. On removing the bandages, such as they were, a mass of filthy rags, the right leg was so amass with gangrene from the putrefying ulcers that it almost came away in their hands.

Shops sprang up only to disappear under the sledgehammer of the new construction plans. The antiseptic smell of the soap factory would neutralise some of the odour coming from the poor homes in the New Street and similar areas.

The hammer of steel against the anvil rang out, as the Bloy's and Joe Day's dealt with the horse and pony traffic of the day. Little herds of horses from various farms would descend outside the barber's shop as they watched the drovers, Willougby and Co. rustle their charges into some kind of order.

Kiddies, armed with buckets, would gather up the residue of the horses discharge on the road, to scamper back home to supply the New Street allotment holders with nutriment for the vegetables, or sell it at 2^d a pail, in time to make first-house at the Kinema.

With beer at 1^d a pint and spirits within access of a customer who had scrimped and slogged only to find it an uphill battle, to finally bury his despair, by drinking to the health of the nation. Women, dragged down by too many children, plus a wayward husband, also would put aside enough money from their taking in washing, to make life seem a little more tolerable. Thus it was that Pimbo had often seen inebriated, swaggering, almost legless men and women, swaying their way from pub to pub, until their money, and the good will of the publican, finally ran out.

Looking out of the barber shop window was, as Albert said, 'Taking a peep at life'. So busy were they, running their own tiny spectrum of existence that they failed to stop and look at themselves. Listening to their conversation, whilst in the barber's chair, was a revelation. Albert felt sorry for the dentist, his customers were not so forthcoming; tense, tight-lipped and certainly not garrulous after a tooth extraction. "They got very little job satisfaction, did the dentists!", thought Albert.

Pimbo was smiling. He was thinking of the barber who, while attending to his customer, would suddenly 'dart' away to jump up and peer out of the window. Maybe, his view of life from the nape of a customer's neck, was hardly enough to whet his appetite on what went on in the outside world.

The Scott family, the younger ones, had a most interesting hobby, in that they angled, and kept livestock. Albert was the one who was more keen on fishing than other pursuits.

Pimbo's next meeting with Jenny dealt with the project so far! In between, the young couple still put their friendship at the top of the list. They both agreed that the venture was something different. It gave them both, a wider view of life, sometimes, they wondered why it was that they seemed always to be holding a curiosity value on what went on in other people's lives.

It was Pimbo who started it all, thought Jenny. Never happy unless fishing around people's lives, it seemed that he felt bonded to do it all. Maybe, it was because of his T.B? One year to live, said the experts! Perhaps Pimbo felt that in such a short time he'd better get cracking and do in a few months, what others might take a lifetime to achieve.

Then, how was it that he managed to drag her in to his new fangled scheme. Well, she loved him, that's how! One day she hoped to marry him, she'd pin him down in the home. She'd have him washing up, changing the kids' nappies, she'd give him, concerning himself with others so much, he wouldn't have time for any such antics.

P.S. Pimbo and Jenny, suddenly realised that Mr Bailey, the ex-librarian of the East Road Reading Room, might well have been the man who had helped Tom Banks with his time capsule venture!

But on the other hand – would she?

Someone had to a write down social history, why bless my soul, thought on Jenny, one day there would be nothing left. Rumours of this coming down, East Road School to go, a great new road going straight along East Road.

She reckoned that barbers' shops would change with new hairstyles coming out from the new films. Even the boys would be going in for a new cut. Already, E. O. Brown at his Fitzroy Street corner shop had introduced them to patent shoes and bow-ties.

The little intimate barber shop might go, just as the little grocer shop on the corner would eventually be pushed out by the large concerns.

"Day dreaming again" said Pimbo, breaking her thoughts. "Not thinking of jacking it in. The barber shop project, I mean – you seem a little concerned"

Jenny laughed "Of course not. Sometimes I think about you doing all this. But the better half of me says, go to it Pimbo, write something that a new generation will savour. Someone should do it, and of course Pimbo, it had to be you!"

"Oh, like that is it, Jenny? Well, maybe you're

right, but let me add something to your 'and of course Pimbo, it had to be you'. I'll say, and what little girl is helping me like mad? And that little girl, Jenny, had to be you!"

There was nothing left for them to do after that – but to kiss!

Cambridge volunteers at Camp in Great Yarmouth 1900
J. Cartwright is the barber.

CHAPTER 12

Peaky White – Barber

Pimbo decided to visit Curly Northfield again. They had progressed quite a bit on the barber project, but Jenny thought it advisable to meet Curly mid-stream and swap ideas.

Curly was all for it. After reading over Pimbo's work so far, he nodded in a way that suggested complete approval, but added a rider. "We need more meaty material, it's not enough to say that so-and-so kept a barber's shop in such-and-such a street. Let's have a story about them, bring 'em to life!"

Glancing across to Jenny, Pimbo smiled. It was all very well for Curly to talk that way – after all, they were only kids still at school, how could they – ?

The little man was reading their thoughts. "I know what you're thinking, but I've been doing a little research myself. It goes a long way back but, thanks to my pal Mr Bailey at the Reading Room on East Road, I've managed to unearth a good deal of 'meaty material', as you call it which should put a little icing on the cake for your project!"

Curly then unfolded a few reams of notepaper on which he'd copied down all the information received from Mr Bailey.

"You'll have to read it yourself, pick out the bits that you think will fill the bill, but I warn you, it'll be hard work because it goes back a very long way, almost as far as when Big Ben was a watch!"

Their friend had slipped in a bit of humour, against their rather downcast looks. Pimbo and Jenny were thinking that it might be too much for them, but Curley's little joke soon got them back into good spirits.

After many hours' work, Pimbo and Jenny knocked into shape, Curley's previous work. The finished product read thus:

Many years ago in Staffordshire Street, No. 27 to be exact, stood a public-house by name 'The White Swan'. It was sited about half-way down, on the left-hand side, looking down from the East Road end. Half of the building jutted out from Gas Lane; a low brick wall blocked out a view into the little bar-room, so that children coming past from Gas Lane, could see only the heads of the drinkers.

At the rear of the pub stood a stable, rather run-down, but good enough for the travellers who stopped at the Inn for food and rest before continuing their journey to London, to rest their horses.

At the side of the yard, well clear of horse-traffic, was a stout wooden type chalet on which

was a sign 'shaving and hair-lopping, other services rendered – as per request.'

The barber's name was Peaky White, a most
noted character of the day. Peaky was a tiny man
with a humpback appearance, not as grotesque as
the Hunchback of Notre Dame, but with so little
difference that at times, Peaky got the benefit of
the doubt.

On race days, punters and racing fraternities,
including riff-raff and road-pads (muggers) would
patronise Peaky's establishment until late hours.

On one particular morning, Peaky was talking
to a man of the turf. "It's up to you, Peaky", the
man was saying, he was a jockey-type fellow, no
bigger than the barber. "It's a handicap, the horse
will be carrying a doddle. He's won over the same
course carrying six pounds more. There's twenty
guineas in it for you, you'd have to be shaving a
few hundred to make that amount of money!" The
barber smiled, rubbing his hands, he took the
racing man into a small cubby hole at the rear of
the shop. Pulling out a large sack he extricated
from it a mass of various coloured hair, much of it
was human hair, but at the bottom was a large
quantity of hair which seemed to have been cut
from a horse mane.

Peaky pointed to the stables, just discernible
from the shed window. "I'm lucky, I slip in at
night, a lump of sugar usually does the trick. I
takes me pick and lops it off, that's why I puts
hair-lopping on my sign, so's you fellows know
what I can do for a poor horse – make it into a
champion overnight!"

The barber laughed at his little joke, then

nudged the man. "Of course, as they leave early in the morning, no-one notices the horse has had one of Peaky's specials – now, what colour will you be wanting? – Take you pick."

The racing man, after fumbling about with different shades of mane, finally chose one with a slight auburn tint. "But how on earth do you manage, mane, fetlocks – aren't you afraid of being tumbled, how do you make it look real? I've heard so many tales of your ringing the changes – one day something's going to go wrong."

"It's you that's taking the chances – not me! I'm like a back street abortionist – it's the gal what takes the chance, anything goes wrong, I deny everything, don't forget that mate. What's the matter with you, getting cold feet? You can call it off, I can get plenty more work from Newmarket. It I relied on shaving and hair-cutting, I'd finish in the workhouse!"

Over a pint at the 'Swan' Peaky soon had his shady customer in a more confident spirit, as he chatted on.

"Human hair, I keep for my little disguises. I'm known all over East Anglia – right up to the smoke. I had Charlie Peace here last year. Casing a big house in Shelford, he was. Wanted a complete change of colouring; I fits him up with a ginger-wig, moustache and side-burns. Never know him you wouldn't, I had to laugh; after the robbery, in the local rag, it said that a man seen outside the house a day before the haul of silver-plate, was reported to have been of ginger-colouring – an arrest would be expected very soon. I'll bet dark-haired Charlie, would laugh his socks off – if he saw that!"

"You'll have to come with me to the Newmarket stables. I daren't risk moving the horse. There's been an inquiry after Sorella won the 1,000 guineas; in the last half-hour it went from 50-1, down to 10–1."

"By the way my name is Croucher, one time jockey, until the stewards warned me off the turf!"

"So, it's another Ringing Job, eh?" queried Peaky "what's the worry, a change is no robbery – they say!"

The racing crook shook his head. "It's had two run-outs this season, the jockey was told to hold back until the big one. Like Sorella. The horse you're ringing, or, should we say disguising for me, will win for sure – but, we must be careful."

Leaving Cambridge an hour after closing time, Peaky and the horse-ringer made their way back to Newmarket, where the barber, complete with special glue, plaster, and the chosen horse-mane loppings, did for the entered horse fake, what make-up artists in the film 'King Kong' did for the amazing gorilla. The horse in question was called 'Ladies Chain.'

Peaky demanded his 20 guineas before leaving the stable.

"The ball's now in your court – I'm not even making a bet on it!"

Arriving back at his little shop, Peaky set about tidying up the cubby-hole containing the lopped off hair of customers and horses. He noticed that he was getting very short of ginger hair clippings, and hoped that some of the red-haired fraternity might begin to patronise his salon a little more than of late.

At that moment a customer walked in. Peaky hadn't seen the man about the Staffordshire Street vicinity. In fact, he seemed far to well attired to come from within a mile of East Road. Carrying a walking stick, with a snake knob, he placed it against the back of the chair, then adjusted his brown brogue shoes to fit in with the position of the barber's chair. At the same time, studying Peaky intently, then gazing around the cramped space, finally, his eyes stared at the cubby-hole.

Positioning himself quickly between the cubby-hole and his client, Peaky asked nervously "What'll it be, Sir. Trim, shave or shampoo?"

"I'll have all three, my man. Seems you have a variation of service – everything but tooth-pulling, leech letting, or bunion bashing, eh, my friend?"

"I haven't the space, Sir. One day, I hope to set up a shop in Burleigh Street, go a bit up-market, if you see what I mean!"

The customer, with Peaky's far from white towel draped around his shoulders, suddenly pulled the day's paper from his pocket. The barber, noticed it as being the 'Westminster Gazette'. He wondered, as the time was only 11 am, how the man had managed to obtain a London paper and yet be in his shop before noon. Peaky also was sweating on why he had chosen his shop, of all places – he felt that the man was on to something – then, too, come to think of it, he did look like a kind of detective!

The man was soon to oblige. Between lathering,

he pointed out, "Seems you barbers have a lot going for you these days. What with Sweeny Todd and his pies, we now have the residue, of hair-cutting, hair dyes, used in the most nefarious of causes. Listen to this, for instance!" He read from his journal:

"The Turf at Doncaster is said to be the place where Lord George Bentinck stabled his sting of racehorses. Last month, he exposed the Running Rein scandal at Derby, proving that the winner was, in fact, a four-year old – disguised with dye and hair loppings from horses manes. And, this too, all laid at the door of the reputable hair establishment in Bond Street, London. A certain Mr Rossi was the proprietor. The case continues"

Poor Peaky, nearly dropped his cut-throat, but somehow kept his cool "They call it ringing, don't they Sir? I read an Edgar Wallace thriller called 'The Ringer' good to!"

"Why is it that you barbers have an interest in horse-racing. They tell me that barbers take in betting slips – a bit dodgy when the police find out, why do you risk it, my man?"

"It's the money, Sir! We get a little commission, it gets customers into the shop. At $1\frac{1}{2}^d$ a shave, and 2^d a haircut round here, we need a little booster in takings, Sir!"

With the completion of his service, the customer paid, tipping the by now sweating-at-the-brow Peaky – with 6^d.

"Enough? I hope to deter you from chancing too much. I'm going to the Newmarket races later today. Any good tips to offer? They tell me that 'Ladies Chain' stands a good chance – nice price, too, twenty-to-one."

Peaky, almost gulped his answer. "No Sir, haven't heard a thing!" After the man had departed, the barber got to thinking. This Rossi chap from Bond Street, London was in deep trouble. The chap must have a lucrative position, attracting the most elite of patrons – and yet he had to indulge in more money making activities. 'The case continues', the fellow read out, and no doubt Rossi would engage the best Q.C. in the business.

But, what chance would Peaky stand. Should Rozzi get 10 years, he'd cop out for a life sentence. Out would come the Charlie Peace story, the biggest rogue in England, and here was the paltry little barber supplying the false moustaches, eyebrows and what have you, a man who stopped at nothing – even murder!

Peaky sank a pint at 'The White Swan'. There was nothing he could do, but wait. First thing in the morning that hand would be on his shoulder. To make things worse it came over on the crystal-set, that 'Ladies Chain' had won at 20-1 odds.

In the morning at 11 am sharp, the same time he'd appeared in the first place, the man arrived. All smiles and beaming.

"Well, Mr White, it all turned out right. My little assumption I mean, not bad twenty-to-one, we all made a packet!"

"We all?" queried Peaky, open mouthed and goggle-eyed.

"I'm Mr Asquith, never told you my name, eh? Thought I was a 'tec didn't you?"

As he spoke, the man tugged away at his

moustache and side-burns which, coming away in his hands, revealed a different personality.

"Lon Chaney, the man with a thousand faces, film's at the Kinema next week. Mr Rozzi, like you, does a good job but I'm afraid hair and dyes will be in short supply. You see, Mr Rozzi is sure to get a long stretch, even with the best of K.C.s. There're many in the Barrister brigade who like a little flutter on the horse – they don't take too kindly to any dirty work in the stables!"

Peaky was a little more composed. "Where's this leave me?"

Asquith smiled kindly and explained. "On my way back from Newmarket, from a deal with Croucher, you see I'm Rozzi's contact man, I stayed the night at 'The White Swan', the stable being close to your shop. Halfway home, I discovered your little handiwork on one of my horses. The next morning my boss Rozzi was arrested. The ringing with 'Ladies Chain' was in the offing – with a good profit. – I wanted to keep it that way."

"I got in touch with Croucher who, as you know, sussed you out. Incidently, I gave him £50 to pay you with – I'll wager he did you down on that – a crafty man is Croucher. I came to see you yesterday to make sure that you hadn't snitched on the deal. Here's £50 for you, a kind of retainer."

Peaky almost snatched the money from Asquith's hand.

"It's the first time I've tried it out on horses – not the real thing I mean, I practiced on rocking-horses to see the effect. Don't you think you'll have to lie low for a bit – ?"

The con-man nodded. "But not for long, there're

hundreds of meetings going on all over the country – I wouldn't cross out the Continent, money to
be made – the sooner the better. I'm thinking of a
nice little house in the country, wife and kids –
you know the stuff! Retire early, that's me."

Peaky argued that he was too down-market
compared to Rozzi with his wider connections in
London. What had a measly cut-and-slash barber
to offer to such an elite ring of shysters?

He was at home in his run-down environment,
Smart's Row, Gas Lane, you didn't see them
mentioned in 'The Tatler'.

But Asquith pointed out that for all Rozzi's
upmarket area – he still was caught! Checking up
in 'The Tatler' put him in touch with many of the
racing clique. He attended their parties and
sussed out the down-at-heel racing stables, ready
to take part in a bit of shady tactics. But with
Peaky as make-up man – the heat would be off, a
kind of Fagin aspect.

Then, too, how close Peaky was to Newmarket!
These arguments caused Peaky to weaken. One
thing though, the little barber had always set his
heart on a shop in Burleigh Street. If Asquith
could pull if off – well then, Peaky was his man!

Thus it was, that the notice a few weeks later,
on Peaky's shop door read: 'This establishment
will shortly move to No. 32, Burleigh Street. New
patrons will be welcomed. Services are per usual.'
Peaky White.

Rozzi, the bent barber was sentenced to 15
years imprisonment. Peaky, flourished in his new
premises; Asquith carried on his nefarious business, finding Peaky an absolute foil against his

genteel good looks and honest appearance – a kind of Beauty and the Beast aspect partnership.

Curley, on reading Pimbo's adaptation of the story was pleased with the effort. "It all happened around 1884!" pointed out their old friend.
"Even to this day, ringing still goes on – it's got round to greyhound and whippet racing – they must use dyes in their case, not enough hair on their sleek bodies to do a Peaky on them."

Pimbo, looking down on to Staffordshire Street from the East Road end, as was his usual wont, tried to visualise the place in the Peaky era. He

Freddy Osbourne's hairdressing salon in Trumpington.

reckoned that at the back of Hammonds's Place, in lieu of 'The White Swan', were little outhouses which once may well have taken part in a few shady tricks. Then, too, the old Popjoy buildings in Gas Lane no doubt could tell a good tale, as could the little maze of tiny houses in Staffordshire Gardens.

The worst that barbers do now, Pimbo hoped, was to take bets. To Pimbo, horse racing was very fascinating, and sometimes alluded to as 'the sport of kings'. If kings could enjoy it – why not the likes of poor old Peaky. He wondered how Peaky got his nick-name. Peaky, meant to look pale, wan, or a little off colour! He supposed, that, as the little hunchback barber rarely tasted the pleasure of the Newmarket downs – well then, that accounted for his being called Peaky.

Jenny couldn't quite share Pimbo's view of the Peaky affair.

"Blinking crooks – the lot of them! It's a good job you've got me as a sweetheart, otherwise you'd finish up behind bars before you reached twenty-one years of age!"

CHAPTER 13

Lady Hairdressers

Following the excitement of the Peaky White saga, Pimbo got down to a little more research into an era not as far back as Peaky's time of living. Jenny would often say "what about the ladies – they cut hair as well, you know – there must be quite a few middle-aged mums, having fond memories of their youth when they tried to look their best for the local dance – or a night at the Beaconsfield!"

Of course, Jenny was right. She remembered her mum, armed with a pair of curling tongs, a terrible scorching smell coming from the kitchen, with dad saying "You should get it done properly – it'll pay you in the end – you've made a right mess of it, haven't you?"

Mum would cry. It was the same when she tried the new fangled hair rinses, either too much, or too little. Poor mum could never get it right.

Getting it right, usually meant a trip to Happy Barratt, or Pinky on Newmarket Road, both within walking distance of each other. Two huge estates had mushroomed up around the area namely the Peverel estate, and the Howard and Keynes Road council homes project.

Gradually, the young girls grew up into fair damsels, very much adored by the boys. And from the films, the youngsters copied the current hair-dos. Home perms, became the vogue, but as with Jenny's mum, and many others, disasters kept Happy and Pinky very busy indeed.

The husband and wife partnership known now as Barratt Happy of 571 Newmarket Road, were a well loved pair giving a wonderful service under the most congenial of atmospheres. In the centre of their front garden was erected a kind of wooden structure advertising their trade – a kind of friendly totempole, amidst the evergrowing population. It seemed, however, that niggardly neighbours or an over bureaucratic dollop of zeal, ended what most people thought was an excellent piece of enterprise, after a terrible time of ration-ing and restrictions. Suffice is to say, the sign had to be taken down so the Barrett's had a wall sign on the side of their house instead – but thanks to their professionalism, the customers increased.

A little way up, on the right-hand side of New-market Road, was the Pink's ladies hairdressing salon. Mrs Pink and daughter were, as the Bar-ratts, an extrovert couple who made many friends, which of course accentuated their trade. Cambridge, at the time was inundated with American troops from the various air-bases around East Anglia.

The Americans, certainly found the Pinks' 'right up their alley' friendly, outgoing. It was rumoured that many a love tryst began at the little establishment where the pretty clientele were eyed up and down by the Yankee beaus. All above board of course, acceptable by boy and girl alike, and keeping trade flourishing at the same time – a real 'On the Town' copy of that famous film, featuring Frank Sinatra and Gene Kelly.

At times, Jenny had visions of going into ladies' hairdressing. In time to come, she reckoned the once dilapidated little stores, pushed out by the larger concerns such as Woolworth's and Marks and Spencer's would be given a new life. It would be like the films depicted in America, new signs and all the new fangled hairlotions. Britain was sure to follow. Out of the hairdressing teaching college would spring eager-beaver youngsters, helped by their parents, setting up little salons all around Cambridge. Ruby's Hair Fashions, Marie Rose Hair Design, Dora's Hairstylists, Betty's Hairtique, Dolly's Hair and Beauty Salon, and such like.

Poor old mum, if she were alive, she would never believe the things they now do with hair. She used odd-ne-dods, a mass of little pieces of rag twisted hopefully around tufts of stringy hair, and when released, she'd stand back and gaze into the mirror – maybe, feeling much better with the new style, hoping that hubby would approve.

Jenny blamed it all on the films, Clara Bow, Jean Harlow, Mae Busch, Nazimova, Laura-la-Plante, mesmerised the growing up teenagers. They too, although miles apart from the screen glory of their idolised heroines, wanted their sweethearts to admire them. They had to save up hard to do it, but 'Amami's night' on its own, couldn't quite make up for the magical touch of a brand new hairstyle.

In a newspaper, Jenny had read that in America the hairstyle craze had reached a dangerous level. A woman, after a special treatment for hair and beauty, was so dissatisfied that she went back to the salon and fired a twelve-bore shot-gun at the hair specialist; luckily she missed, but had to pay damages for the cracked mirrors and bottles of hair-lotions that had received the brunt of her wrath.

Jenny smiled as she looked up at Pimbo, seemingly content with his usual 'short back and sides' from Albert Scott. I suppose one day, he'd settle in for singe, shampoo and hairstyling, all in one sitting – maybe he'd have to become a little more mature for that improvement!

As Jenny was saying "All at once, came a surge of ladies hairstyles taking precedence over many other domestic issues!"

A certain ladies' hairstylist hit the headlines as a bolt from the blue – he was known as 'Teasy Weasy'.

This gentleman had the women eating from the palm of his bejewelled fingered hands. In next to no time, he was in the money; money which brought him a string of race horses and enabled him to open new salons all over the country. His face was featured in every newspaper, foreign or otherwise. With the coming into the homes of television, 'Teasy Weasy' became a household name. He was given a series by the T.V. moguls which led to many lonely wives fantasising with him as their lover.

All this brought to bear the real significance that ladies placed on their appearance concerning hairstyling. It gave women a new impetus against male dominance. Undoubtedly, films had a primary role in the sudden transformation from accepted mundane hairstyling to that of the new breathtaking hair-dos. What Mrs Shilling did for hats at the Ascot races, 'Teasy Weasy' did for hairstyles, which promped the ladies to spend more money on their hair than on exotic Shilling creations – they simply left off their hats!

In the midst of all the adulation and 'hair raising' international renown, poor 'Teasy Weasy' developed cancer of the jaw. During this session of pain and many operations Teasy Weasy showed a quality of character in line with the quality of his artistic creations. Pictures of his distorted face appeared in many journals, but 'Teasy Weasy' battled against the disease, and with the help of distinguished surgeons and, no doubt a great deal of money he came through in the end, with a fresh flock of admiring women clientele.

All this brought a spate of 'Teasy Weasy' look alikes, but this brave man will go down in the annals of ladies' hairstylists as the pioneer of it all – as Pimbo remarked "He deserved it – no one seems to have done much for us men!"

Pimbo was getting back to more research into the male barbers. Arthur Whitehead, a cousin of the Scott regime, started up in Newnham during the early 1900s, closed during the 1914 Great War, to set up once more on returning from the fray. He was most noted for the hairstyle of his

very own choice, that of a kind of military quiff, a
lock of hair plastered down on to the forehead.
Also, he never worked without wearing an immaculate white apron.

His little shop was situated a short distance
from the Mill. Arthur was a real shaving man –
well before intricate hairstyling came into vogue,
he carried on his barbering days well into the
1930 era. In those days, Arthur's little establishment must have presented a rather incongruous
sight; Newnham with its Ridley Hall, young lady
students, strolling along its lanes, with a goodish
sprinkling of college dons adding to the academic
scene.

In later years, the coming of the Labour Exchange must have restored the working class
equilibrium.

Arthur Whitehead's barbering service continued after his retirement. It was taken up by a
member of the Hairdresser's Federation who plied
his trade in a private house close by the Newnham
Institute building. This barber, perhaps seeking
more trade than sleepy Newnham could offer,
tried his fortunes by moving out to Snettisham.
But it was to no avail, the reluctant barber
returned, finding the other fields were no greener
than those of dear old Newnham!

Another old Federation barber was Mr A.W.
Franscis of 18 Lensfield Road. His was a very tiny
shop close by the Oak Pub, a habitat of many
Irishmen. He was a small, dignified man whose
mother apparently insisted on being the cashier.
He used to tell a good tale concerning the Irishmen that frequented his shop, one of which, went:

Defending the fact that Irish people were supposed to be a little eccentric, the half-drunk boyo
proclaimed that God said, after making the Irish
"well, there's you are now, keep on acting daft,
until I git's back to ye!"

On Mr Francis' retirement, the shop was taken
over by his grandson, a Mr Underwood, to finally
come under the demolition hammer.

Pimbo then ferretted out a barber who officiated
in Norwich Street. This was in the all shaving era
and the hard working barber had to fight against
the biggest mass of demolition ever seen in Cambridge. In the derelict spaces left by the de-
molishers, the little man hung on, until age, and
the stress of finding new premises finally took its
toll.

Then we have Frank Edwards. Another Federation man, Frank's shop was in Mill Road
almost opposite the now Broadway shopping
centre. This barber was a fine billiards player,
giving close games to the best of players including
Bert Charge. Frank's shop was in the centre of the
railway worker's domain, no doubt the kindly
barber did much towards making the appearance
of the rail workers as smart as indeed they were,
in those times of dedicated and loyal Union men.

Pimbo was remembering another Irish joke
from A. W. Francis' long list of anecdotes, that of
the Irish motorist who took his car in for a
'service' and got caught between the church doors!
There was no doubt that barber shops were a real
breeding ground for tall tales.

Jenny was working hard on getting together
their work on the interesting project. A girl friend

of Jenny's who was taking a course at the Pit-
man's School of Typing, a good deal of practice by
working on the manuscript and typing it into
numbered pages. So far it had been great fun,
with people cooperating wonderfully when it came
for them to give out a few nostagic memories of
the many barbers of the day. It was like asking
the way, really, in a district unfamiliar to you –
people seemed to enjoy showing you the way. Now
and then, the young couple would take a short
respite by going to the flicks. The Kinema of
course was Pimbo's favourite, always cowboys,
but Jenny liked the quiet walk across Jesus Green
up to the Tivoli. They seemed to show gentler
films there, or else a little further along to the
Rendezvous in Magrath Avenue.

But, trust Pimbo, it was soon back to the
project, prying out more information. Jenny reckoned that her boyfriend was practically dreaming
about barber shops. She pulled his leg once, by
saying, "I'll bet you wake up in a real lather!"

Dear old Curly Northfield was taking snap
peeps at their work. He seemed well pleased and
like Jenny, warning Pimbo not to become too
earnest – things would work out, he'd say. But as
Pimbo would say "The field is wide open, very
soon those little shops, like the corner-stores, will
disappear and the old Federation barbers will go
with them!"

Curly surprised them by coming straight back
with an anecdote he'd just remembered. This
concerned a barber in Chesterton, having as a
customer a certain Joe Bates. Joe, a first world
war veteran had lost a leg at Mons, but was a very

A small view of the Cartwright shop, embracing Verlander's famous "little Kettle" (Mr Verlander is seen tending his stock).

determined man, walking great distances. At the time, he worked for a certain Mr Oppenheim who was well versed in the polishing of stones and certain glassware. Joe, undoubtedly, had learned a few wrinkles from his old boss.

In the last war 1939–1945, a great deal of research was being done to perfect the lenses, which were so much in demand for binoculars, range-finders, predictors for searchlights and many others. One day, Joe Bates was watching a certain professor struggling away at polishing a new lens.

Joe stepped forward. "Mr Oppenheim would tell

you at once, that you are going about it the wrong way – you polish as though the lens were as hard as a diamond – which, it is not."

Joe then demonstrated, by means of well distributed common spittle, plus a specific method of two-way polishing, how to bring the lenses to a perfect lustre.

From then on, this method, altered of course a little technically, was used on all wartime instruments.

The barber pointed out, that Joe's past employer, was Carter & Jonas of Peas Hill. At the time, Joe lived at 38 Cam Causeway.

CHAPTER 14

The London Barber

Pimbo received good news one morning. The summer school holidays had just begun. Through distant relatives on his father's side, Pimbo had a 'near' uncle living in London, who of all things – was a barber!

To Pimbo's delight, on the strength of his barbers' project, the uncle had invited him down to stay with him for two weeks. It was a heaven sent chance for Pimbo to compare a London barber's life to that of his Cambridge peers.

Luckily, too, Jenny was going away into the country for a spell, which would make their parting a little more tolerable.

The uncle lived in the Highbury portion of N.W. London. He had a room above his tiny shop which was situated in a sleazy side street off Blackstock Road. To Pimbo's pleasure, at the bottom of the road, was the Finsbury Park Empire theatre and at the crest of the road was the Arsenal's Highbury Stadium.

Mr Adams, the uncle who had been so kind in his offer to Pimbo, met the boy at the tube-station, then walked with him to his shop in Fairburn Street. It proved to be a tiny place indeed, just a little bigger, thought Pimbo, than old Chinner's in Chesterton.

"I set up after coming out of the Army" said the barber. "You can call me uncle Sid. Me old dad had the place, and when mum died, the owner took off the side of the house with the three rooms, to let to a young couple, leaving me with the shop and the room up top – it was that, or get out!"

"You never married?" queried the boy.

"Not the marrying sort! Me mum and dad were always rowing, hammer and tongs. I saw a lot of men double-crossing their wives and vice versa, so I pockets me little bit of savings to put in a few extra bits in the shop. Dad had thrown a 'lucky seven', so the place was mine."

In the salon itself, which seemed bigger than it looked from outside, at the end was a small bed, cushioned to take the seats of the customers. The barber's chair was quite formidable, no doubt Sid had put some of his Army gratuity into buying that; there were four chairs at the other end of the salon, close to the door.

Sid glanced across to Pimbo, who, at that moment was viewing the bed. "I got that in for the apprentice boy, run away from home he had. But trade didn't quite cover his keep, then I knew that one day he'd slope off again, so it made it easier for me to get rid of him – he was no good with a cut-throat anyway! By the way, the bed is yours now, I'll make it up with clean linen. I can't have the neighbours talking – with you sleeping upstairs!"

Next morning, which was a Saturday, the customers began popping in. Mostly, they were fairly old men, shaving being the primary order of the day: Sid told Pimbo to sit and take note. Should he get too busy, well, then, the boy could do a bit of lathering.

One old fellow was talking to Sid. "Glad to get out of the house, I was. Rowing like hell they was. Seems that when the old gal died, one of her sisters was paying in a penny a week against her death, the other paid in two per week to the Hearts of Oak. One got £8, the other £16. Then they'd say 'you're only waiting for mum to die and get that money!' Then up comes the eldest son and claims the lot. Then, there's a real barney, because a sister in Australia demands a share of the money. I reckon them that pays in over the years, should get the money – they say the law's looking into it – I reckon the eldest son gets away with too much!"

To relieve the situation, Pimbo picked up a broom and swept up a few loose hairs on the floor, along with two empty woodbine packets, he dumped it into the waste bin.

As he sat listening, Pimbo felt that he was getting a first-hand look into the problems of the Londoners, not that much different from those in Cambridge, but somehow he felt an alien.

One old chap was spouting "We're better off than we were. I can remember my old mum and dad earning 2^d for seven gross of match boxes, made 'em up they did. Even when you got wages,

you had to pay back a few shillings you'd bor-
rowed in the week. We never had Unions in those
days, some days, day after day, I never earned a
penny because of wet weather!"

Sid's next in the chair was adding to the misery:
"People aren't so friendly. They can't afford to
come and talk to you. Some have got on better
than you, and can't be bothered to know you.
People used to say 'Goodnight' when you passed
them in the street, and all that sort of thing!"

Another followed with: "Nowadays, it's all white
weddings. We went back to work when we were
married. We never hired a big hall like they do
now; we used to empty all the furniture and use
the house. There weren't many white weddings in
those days. My mother got married in a mauve
bonnet and a paisley shawl, me dad just about
managed a suit. Each of my sisters had grey
weddings – but, they were just as pure as those
that had white." He went on. "They respect their
dead better today. In the old days they'd stop at a
half-way house at the burial. Most would drink
more than they should, then they'd start arguing
over the things in the mothers' homes. In many
cases there would be fights on the way back!"

During a lull, Sid made Pimbo a cup of tea
"Don't let 'em get you down boy. When you get old,
you seem to go on a bit about the old days –
sometimes for the better, sometimes worse. I get
used to it, sort of stops me worrying about not
getting spliced. I can live all my worries concerning married life through them – expiation they
call it, I think! That's what comes of being a
barber."

As the door began to open, Sid smiled across at the boy. "This'll be old Bill Jones, he's a widower, 73 years old – you listen, tells me all he does from the moment he wakes up! Sure enough it was Bill. Sid got him going straight away for Pimbo's benefit. "What've you been up to today then, Bill?" Bill obliged enthusiastically: "got up at 7.30 am made a cup of tea. 8 am started to clear up. Cleared the fireplace out, I had the sweep coming between 9.30 and 10 am, they're very strict on time. At 9 am, had some bread and marmalade, and the sweep came at 9.45 am. He stayed about 20 minutes, cost me 5/-; I then swept up and got out at 11.15 am. Got my paper 'News Chronicle' and 20 Woodbines. Then I bought a loaf of bread 8^d, bacon 1/8, 4 eggs 1/2 and some marge ½lb 9^d – 4/3 the lot. I fancied a bit of fish for my tea, so went across to the fish shop and bought a kipper, and bit of plaice 2/- the lot. Won a bit on the football sweep, thought I'd treat myself. Well, here I am having a trim and shave. After I leave here I shall go home, light me fire, have me kipper and plaice, and a nice Woodbine, then wash up and clear the place up. Then I'll listen to the wireless, cup of cocoa, and two biscuits and bed, about 10 pm roughly speaking, Sid!"

Sid smiled as he watched Pimbo's earnest little face taking it all in. Bill hadn't forgotten Pimbo. "Nice lad, you've got there Sid. New apprentice eh? Seems to pay attention as to what's going on!"

If Jenny had been there, Pimbo reckoned she'd have said, "You can say that again, Bill!"

On the following Saturday, Sid closed his salon at mid-day. Arsenal were playing at home; a few

weeks before their match with Everton, Arsenal
had completed the first £10,000 transfer deal by
allowing their star player, David Jack to move on
to Bolton Wanderers. Sid reckoned there could be
trouble from the unruly fans should Arsenal get
beaten; and they passed by his shop on the way to
the Finsbury Park tube.

In the afternoon the barber and Pimbo sat
talking. The boy reckoned there was little difference between Sid's customers and the Cambridge
ones. Somehow, however, he thought there
seemed to be a stronger bond between Cockney
families, than those of the Cambridge people.
Whilst being serviced by Sid, they would talk
more readily of their next-of-kin, going back a
good few years, even into the great, great grandfather era.

There was the exception. The friendly barber
told Pimbo of an elderly spinster who had nursed
her frail mother for many years, hardly making
contact with the outside world. On her mother's
death the daughter arranged everything concerning burial procedures. There were no relatives, no
next of kin, the only people present at the funeral
were the daughter and minister.

On the Monday, things soon got back to normal.
Pimbo had managed to obtain a good deal of
information about the barber's patrons, his note-
book was crammed ready for Jenny's sorting out.
He found out that rents varied between 5/7^d to
12/6. Coal was 7/6 per hundredweight, a loaf of
bread 8^d. Toast with marmalade was the favourite
breakfast, but on Sunday, bacon and eggs were
managed by most families.

5/- seemed to be the most popular monetary gift for presents etc. Stewing meat for a family meal ran out at 1/6^d.

On one funeral, the insurance paid for the actual burial but, at the end, the whole family had to call at the insurance office to collect the residual sum of £2.15s. This was to be divided by the family but, rightly so, it was given to the bereaved widow. Then a collection was made to buy a headstone – it cost £24.

War widows would have rosettes in their hats, black with white in the centre. There would be three months full mourning; young children would wear white frocks with a black sash or bow, for 2 months.

Sid told the boy that the widows married again as quickly as possible after the funeral, a few had already lined up their spouse before the funeral. In those days, there was no widow's pension so they either had to go out to work or find a husband quickly.

The barber seemed surprised that Pimbo and Jenny had taken it on their young shoulders to write notes about barbers, their shops, and the people that patronised them. He agreed, however, that there was something completely different about a barber shop. He reckoned that a man, reclining back in a chair, neck rest and all, perhaps coming out of his house having had a row with the missus, could well regard it as an opportunity for reflection. The women, under a hairdryer would have a magazine handed her – but a man would have to rely on his own thoughts. Then, too, a man was different, reckoned Sid, never really got out of the little boy stage. He felt it as soon as he wrapped a towel around the man's neck or, held a mirror to the nape of his neck – there was that certain look that came over his face. A customer, under the spell of a barber's routine, would practically confess to murder. It was better than alcohol, to loosen a man's tongue!

One day an old man was talking about birthdays. On account of what he had to say, Pimbo reckoned it hadn't been quite like that in Cambridge. It seemed that an aunt of his, 78 years of age, had told him the following: "I've never had such a birthday, I wasn't expecting it either. My eldest daughter took a place in Drayton Gardens, near Holloway Road. She got the room all done up, and then we all trundled along – all the family, and them next door. There must have been nigh on 50 of us. We had a lovely tea, beautiful cake, they couldn't blow all the candles out. Then we had a right old booze-up. We sang songs, I sang like Billy-ho, some of us finished up under the table, I can tell you but, 'twas all in good fun and no fighting!

Pimbo was enthralled with the stories coming from the old men. Sometimes, when they looked across to him they'd say "Bugger, boy, you ain't bin born yet. In my day, families thought more of each other than they do now." Then they would rattle on: Family teas were often held on weekends, turning into sing songs and parties. Twenty to 30 relatives would, at times, meet in a pub. A large table of men, and a separate table for women. All the husbands buy the wives beer, and take turns to pay on what was known as a 'call'.

Holidays were different. Some families spent a whole month in the hop fields of Kent. One family had what they called a bungalow hut, where they would spend a week outside London. One old man said "there were usually 10–12 of us, I slept in a single bed with my grandson – he'd say 'mind you don't kick me out of bed – grandad.'

Pimbo, at the end of Sid's day, would muse over the wonderful experiences he'd overheard and ponder over the fact that in barber shops all over the world, those kind of memory stirring tales went on. He was glad he'd started this project, as the old fellow had said "Pimbo, you ain't bin born yet!"

To Pimbo's surprise, Sid had prepared a few notes of his own, apparently fired by the boys enthusiasm he had written down an excerpt from a report in a local journal of a special outing to Brighton for the day. It seemed that the writer of the account had mingled well with the participants to give a word of mouth report.

About 400 old people from Finsbury and Holloway combined in eleven coaches went to Brighton for the day. It was cold and grey. A woman of eighty, although sick the previous day, still turned up for the outing. They all assembled on the end of the central pier to have lunch in one of the splendid pavilions. There was a good deal of horse play, teasing, and flirting. Talk circled around infirmity, ill health, and the inadequacy of pensions. Proud stories were told about the kiddies. Banter ran as follows:

"You thought I was going to run after you, didn't you?"

"You don't want to put your best things on when you go larking about in Brighton. I've got my old whistle and flute" (suit).

"I told 'em my daughter doesn't keep me. I go halves, I told 'em. Halves with the rent, halves with the coal and everything. It's terrible the cost of food, isn't it? All your money goes on the table, and me 76 years old."

"If I was 80, I'd find it hard getting about, she weren't well yesterday you know!"

"If we hadn't a smile for one another, we wouldn't be much good."

"All the people where I live, had a cheery word for me, Bob the dustman, they all knew me then. But, they've grown out of knowledge now, the young 'uns. When they see an old age pensioner they think you want something off them. I have one old friend left, he's 80, we meet once a week at the top of the street. We have one brown ale each, that's all we can afford."

One of Sid's customers was talking about retirement. He reckoned that very few men could afford to retire, unless they were too infirm to work. He himself was forced to give up work drawing trolleys in a meat factory. The work was getting too heavy for him. "A day seemed a week to me. I tried getting a lighter job, although I was 65 I told them I was only 55. I tried 40 offices and such-like in London, but without success. They'd say 'Are you sure you're not 65? I said 'Why ask all these questions – give a man a chance!' But I knew they'd find out by my Insurance cards. I knew a chap who worked until he was 80 as a shop assistant then, after the sack, he started at another shop until he was 87."

The old man went on. "The day I got the sack, that was a day that was, me wife was crying, me grown up kids were crying. I had the hump, I didn't know what to do. All I could see was those four walls. I used to earn £8 with me long hours, and give me wife £5. Now I can't stand anybody a drink. I'll tell you this – the happiest time of my life was when I was at work, I used to be good at all types of sport, now I can't even walk properly, my feet go flop, flop, flop, just like that, – flop, flop, flop!"

Sid told Pimbo afterwards, that a widower received £2.10 per week on retirement. Married couples £4.40.

Some men on retirement received £3.10–£4, but this included perhaps retirement pensions. national assistance and various gratuities.

The wife would give back to her spouse 2/6–5/- according to the amount she received. It was accepted by the men that the wife would hold the purse strings.

One evening, Mr Adams got cross with Pimbo. "You're looking pale, too pale for a kid your age. You've been sitting here for nearly two weeks just listening to tales of woe and poverty. It ain't fair for a kid – O.K, you and Jenny are on this project – but, Pimbo, you must have a break. I'm closing the shop for two days, we'll look around the place. I'll take you to Collins Music Hall in Islington, you'll like that – come to that, I could do with a breather myself!"

Pimbo agreed, sometimes he wondered if it was all fair to Jenny. Then, on the other hand, if you

want to get on you've got to start somewhere. He
wanted one day to be a real writer, get books into
people's homes that they could enjoy. His stay
with Sid, had taught him a lot, mainly that
Londoners had that little something different.
Take the old fellow working until he was 87, shop
assistant at that. Then, too, it was good to know
that barbers were the same all over the kingdon,
just shaving, cutting and styling hair – and above
all else, just listening.

Sid kept to his word. That evening they went
down to Islington and saw George Robey, known
as the Prime Minister of Mirth. He wore a little
bowler hat, carried a stick, and made everyone
laugh their headsoff. The friendly barber then
took Pimbo round to see other barber shops. They
were huge compared to Sid's little place. Some
had two sections, one for hairdressing, the other
for snacks and drinks. Others where they wore
very flashy bow-ties, and the shirt bands which
you see in the American movies. There were all
kinds of facilities, hand drying, soap dispensers, it
all seemed like a film set to Pimbo. He asked Sid if
he had heard about Rossi the crook barber. All
London knew, well before he was arrested. You
don't make a fortune out of a barber's shop unless
you're a 'Teasy Weasy'. I reckon a lot goes on in
some of the places we've seen – horse racing, at
times, lends itself to a bit of double-dealing!

So, on a high note, Pimbo left the Finsbury Park
area to travel back to Cambridge and his Jenny.
Thanking Sid for his kindness, he promised that
Sid's name would be in the book. The barber
invited him back – "At anytime!"

Mr Albert Scott, 169 East Road, Cambridge at work in his salon (Cambridge's oldest working barber).

CHAPTER 15

Dear Old Frank – Mill Road Barber For 40 Years

The next barber on Pimbo's list was Frank Edwards of 191 Mill Road, on the corner of Thoday Street. Frank's wife, Joan, was in charge of the Ladies' hairstyling and cutting side of the business. Frank's initial contribution to the research was that in accordance with most barber's statements, the trade was not a lucrative one and it was indeed, a very hard working effort to obtain a living. The barber, like most, did a fair amount of shaving, beard trimmings, but pulled only two teeth during his sojourn as a master-barber.

Two factors in causing a poor week's takings were a visit by the Circus, and the Fair. Customers delayed a haircut in order to treat their children to the annual event. Another bad time for trade was three weeks before Christmas, mainly because customers wanted to look their best for the holiday.

Frank would tell how his thumb (showed scarring) to this day, owing to his testing the sharpness of his open razor. He also bemoaned the lack of a real good honing base. Travelling reps would leave one behind for him to try, and on their next monthly visit, should the honing block not be to his liking, they would leave yet another to be sampled. Frank reckoned that only a few had the unoxidised flat surface, combining a certain carbon element which would hone a razor to his liking.

Mr Edwards, carried on business with his wife at the same shop for 42 years, having originally served an apprenticeship in Rugby, prior to his launching out on his own. On apprentices, Frank pointed out that very few actually paid a premium, but as he put it, he paid them each week on what he thought they were worth. On some weeks, he had very little left over for himself.

Frank's wife Joan, butted in here by telling of her nightmarish effort in teaching a left handed girl apprentice to do hairstyling. Joan reckoned, as did Frank, that using a mirror to counteract the left hand enigma, was the best way to achieve this teaching and learning. Frank was a very fine follower of the arts and tells a little story of a show in Cambridge called 'The Naughty Girls'. It seemed that in Thoday Street, theatre artistes were found lodgings. Two young performers used his shop to purchase matches and razor blades. This was in 1948, and to Frank's surprise the girls took part in nude shows!

The question of selling matches and cigarettes cropped up. The barber pointed out that he actually lost money on the sales, because of his outside machines. Frank would, before loading up the machine with cigarettes (Players, then were 11½^d for 20) have to cut a slit in the packet, in order to insert a half-penny, which would constitute the change from the 1/- slot machine. However, people would file down foreign coins to fit the machine, thus, diddling Frank out of cigarettes and the ½^d in change!

One of his regular customers was the doorman at the New Theatre, before its sad decline. Resplendent in a military style uniform, the commissionaire would tell Frank of the variance in the manner of some of the show people.

Evelyn Laye, to him was tops. She had a kindly word for everyone. Sadly, Max Miller, contrary to his breezy style on stage, was very different in the bar of the theatre. He was surly and ready to argue with anyone. Davy Kaye, a pint sized comedian, still going strong in Benny Hill's shows, was a lovable man on and off the stage. As was Benny Lee, at that time a crooner as popular as Bing Crosby.

Frank expounded many little traits of barber's, expected by the very poor neighbourhood. It was quite common for them to lend money, never charge interest! Never gossip, but have a ready ear the worst. He reckoned that some customers told him the most confidential secrets which, he was sure, they would never dare tell anyone else.

Horse-racing tips were begged of, although Frank himself never indulged in the pastime.

On the introduction of the safety razor, trade did not go down, because most of his customers were not the 'easy shaves' (these customers managed it themselves) but wore tough grizzled beards, the likes of which he could well do without. In fact, although the Palm Olive soap people actually gave away a razor with every bar sold, in the end customers didn't bother to accept them, but gave them back to the barber.

Frank pointed out the difficult men for hair cutting. These customers usually wore a hat or cap pulled well down to their ears. On removing the head-gear, a deep cut ridge around the bottom of the head would present itself. This proved very difficult to cut into and Frank would sometimes, at an especially difficult one, ask, "Are you a left hand, or right hand thread?" as he was about to take of the customer's hat.

Frank interposed here to point out that part of the reason for a barber's popularity was the actual combing of the hair. A customer would say how soothing and relaxing it was. Frank noticed the change of expression of the customer's face as soon as he began combing. He reckoned at times, he was sure that he could send the customer off into a trance, similar to that of an hypnotist.

Frank told a little tale about the six records he was for ever playing on his old gramophone to amuse his customers in the shop. A certain old chap, it could have been George Pope, used daily to parade past Frank's shop trundling a pram on which rested a gramophone. The same old tune was played over and over again, until an exasperated Frank said to his appentice Jimmy Dye "Go and give him my six records, and tell him to change the tunes each day!" Frank was intending to buy a fresh supply of records for himself.

However, after a week or so he realised that he was still having to listen to the same old tunes he already had been playing to his customers. Of course in those days, lack of traffic made it quite possible for the gramophone tunes to permeate into the shop on a warm day!

Jim Dye, the apprentice boy, stayed with Frank from a short-trousered boy of 14 years for a number of years. On leaving, Jim opened up a shop of his own in Histon. Jim died at the age of 57 years of cancer.

At this Joan, Frank's wife, told of the left-handed girl apprentice who stayed with her for nine years before finally moved to Brighton, but still keeps in contact with her ex-boss.

Back to Frank, who stated that the long hair vogue affected trade a little, as in lieu of weekly cuts, this broadend out to a monthly trim. But styling and shampooing made up for this loss of the short-back-and-sides brigade.

Frank also remembered a young student, who came into the shop regularly for his hair to be 'set'.

In 1930, Frank told of the Proprietor of the Del-monte salon in Petty Cury, presumably a Mr Robert Alderton, sending him a letter to request his support in founding the National Hairdressers Federation – a kind of Trade Syndicate. Of the many letters sent out, he received only two replies, that from Frank and one from Mr Asbury Sr of Trinity Street.

The fact that no ladies joined, was due to the rule of 'No Ladies' which the venue for the monthly meetings in the 'Still and Sugar Loaf' a noted pub-cum restaurant, strictly adhered to. To allow the lady-hairdressers their say in the matter, a new meeting place was found in a large house in Hills Road. After this a strong Federation of both classes was formed. Frank of course going down in history as a Founder Member.

Joan's side of the business flourished, giving her many reputable clientele. One of these, was Irene Flanders, daughter of Flanders the Chemists of Mill Road. Irene became a famous contralto, singing in concerts all over the United Kingdom. At a period when she was seriously ill with broncho-pneumonia, straw was actually laid on the road outside her house to silence the rumble of traffic which, with her ailment, exascerbated the pain. Such was Irene's regard for Joan; a silver wedding ring, heirloom of the family, was given by her to Joan, in recognition of her excellent service. Mr Flanders, the father, was a well loved figure in Mill Road. The poorer families looked upon him as their doctor; he would make up special potions to cure their maladies, most of which always worked.

Frank went on to talk about more shop characters. One, was known as the 17lb baby. This man, although not unusually big, would boast of his weighing 17lb at birth. Getting a little fed up with the bragging, one man interjected "Your poor old mum must have been glad to have got rid of you at that weight!"

Joan weighed in with one of her own stories. In the impoverished areas of Mill Road, butter was a rarely used commodity owing to its price, margarine became the staple diet of most of her customers. One lady, however, would often voice out "I can honestly say that margarine has never passed my lips!"

One bored customer replied "Do you do any cooking?"

At the affirmative reply, she asked "what do you use for fat?"

The answer was 'margarine!' at which she was asked.

"So you don't eat your own cooking?"

The lady hotly replied "Of course I do!"

The bored lady quickly slipped in "Well then, margarine has passed you lips, my girl!"

Joan added, "The boasting customer was always called, after this incident, 'Margarine Maggie'.

Another customer of Frank's was the horse-van driver to Ellis Merry a well known business man at the time, who also ran an undertaker's concern as well as owning property. The horse-van was used for furniture removals taking the driver around many parts of the countryside. Ellis fell foul of the van driver's wife, because her husband was never at home to receive his wages; in the end, the wife insisted that Ellis pay her during her hubby's absence. Poor hubby, as soon as he finished one job, he would get a message to carry on to another destiny; Ellis would get the message through to some spot where the horse-van would pass sometimes it might be two weeks, or more, before the driver reached home.

Tom Amey, mayor at the time, John-De-Boldt Sr, the noted Dutchman dentist, and Len Stearn the chemist, were among Frank's customers.

Another character was the chauffeur of Sir

Edmund Gray. The chauffeur was a regular customer of Frank's and told many stories concerning
the wealth of his employer, one which was: Sir
Edmund was due to go to France on a big confer-
ence. Although owning a beautiful Daimler car he
decided it unethical to be seen in France with a
British car. The chauffeur was given orders to
visit a car works in Paris, and pick out their best
model for the journey – at a princely sum!

Sir Edmund owned racehorses and often went
to Ireland in order to follow his nags. It was
rumoured that his lordship on going through a
peasant village with his entourage of sleek cars
caused the simple folk to run indoors and peep
through the curtains at what they deemed 'such
an amazing spectacle'.

The chauffeur explained bitterly to Frank, that
despite Sir Edmunds being a racing man he never
voluntary gave his driver a racing tip. One day,
out of complete frustration, the chauffeur asked
"Have we a chance, today, Sir?" Although the
reply was "Not an earthly, James!" Sir's horse
won at 10–1.'

During a little lull in the old master-barber's
tales, he confided to Pimbo that he was, he
thought, the first barber to obtain a hydraulic
chair. In turn, Joan said she was the first on the
scene to use electric hair clippers. Sunday mornings was used up by scrubbing out the shop and
cleaning all the instruments and paintwork.

Returning to customer characters, Frank
brought in Jack Custerson, one of Kelsey Ker-
ridge's master craftsman. Jack was given the task
by Kelsey, who himself was an expert builder-

joiner, making a set of gates made out of actual black bog oak, which had been ordered for a college in Australia. Frank pointed out to Pimbo, that the bog oak must have been the most durable of wood. Jack had told him that it had been buried until it almost reached the fossil stage of coal.

The gates were loaded on board a ship and Jack was able to present them to the college concerned during an almost civic reception a very proud moment for Jack – mused the old barber!

Frank finished his discourse with Pimbo by saying that he had not begrudged a day of his barbering career, as did his wife Joan confirm her agreement. He had serviced three generations of families. Pointing out that on several occasions he was able to tell grandsons about their fathers' fathers. Things they'd never heard before, kind things of course, but little tales that only belong in a barber's shop. In the latter years, both Frank and Joan feel that the chromium-plated up-market salons gradually pushed them out. The youngsters had judged them as 'past it'. Trade gradually waned, old faces disappeared, so the barbering pair finally called it a day to retire into a nice little bungalow. As Frank called it, "A nice backwater in Button End, Harston."

Lower ground floor of Joshua Taylor's new men's salon in the 1930s. Note prices: Haircut 10^d, (5p); boys 8^d, (4p); Shampoo 1/-, Mud pack 3/6. The well known Dominic is now in charge, giving equally good service – but, of course, with higher tariff.

CHAPTER 16

The Travelling Barber

When Pimbo next met Jenny she was tying up a few loose ends on some of the barbers already mentioned in the project. Bill Kemp, the well loved barber of Fiztroy Street, had, added to his research, information to the fact that his gangrenous leg might have been caused by his habit of pressing the leg up against the back of the barber's chair. Customers it seemed could feel the pressure slightly on their backs. Ray Newman, a barber in the City centre told of his offering to run Bill's shop during his stay in hospital, Ray was a close relative of Bill. Also, it wasn't that Bill was stubborn about his going in to hospital, it was because poor old Bill had a fear of going into hospital which, in those days, was shared by many others.

In confirmation of Bill's habit of pressing his leg against the chair, when Ray helped out in sorting out the ex-barber's effects, he found that the fabric of the chair had worn so thin, that one more day of Bill's working would have seen the back of the chair collapse!

Ray added another little tale to Bill Kemp's career as a barber. Bill's shop at the end of Fitzroy Street attracted a lot of racegoers who, on a good day would spend a little extra on grooming, at the same time telling Bill of their racing wins. One day in a packed shop a man came in, almost in tears, bemoaning the fact that he'd lost everything at Newmarket races and had nothing more to live for. Bill, to spare his customers more lamentations suggested that the man came back when he was less busy. The customer, however, said he'd stay because he only wanted to purchase an open razor. At this, Bill couldn't get him out of his shop quickly enough with the words following the unhappy man, "Away with you. You're not cutting your throat in my shop!"

As his leg grew worse Bill, although he rode a cycle, was seen merely pushing his bike and just leaning on it to propel him along. On Sundays, Bill would visit any sick customer to shave or trim at a relatively low cost. A character sadly missed in the world of scissor and comb!

Jenny, as though wishing to make up for absence during her boy's session in London, showed Pimbo a cutting from the local paper, it read: Headlines 'Scalped!' Then to follow:

A teenager, 'scalped' after being offered a free hairdo, vowed that she would stay away from school until her hair grows back. It seemed that she was stopped in the street and asked: "Do you want a free hair cut?" She went to a nearby salon and was talked into having a trim – lasting two and a half hours!

The girl had brown shoulder length hair with curls before the snip. "I was stopped outside Harrods by a girl in her twenties. My friend was keen to take up the offer, so I went with her to the salon. After a while, another girl said to me. 'You need a trim, the ends of your hair are really dry.' I said 'no thanks – I'm happy with my hair how it is'. But the girl was very persistent. She said 'I won't do more than a trim!' I weakened and that so-called trim lasted two and a half hours. I couldn't stop her, she didn't understand what I said – she was Japanese. When I looked in the mirror I could have died!" The nightmare haircut was done at Sanrizz in London's Brompton Road. The girl finished almost bald!

Manager Tony Rozzi, said "We run a school and have over 200 models, how my girls look for them is up to them."

Asked whether his company has a code on recruiting models, Mr Rozzi hung up. The National Hairdresser Federation said "This is an appalling way of looking for models!"

Pimbo, who has a keen memory, looked up as Jenny finished reading out the cutting "Rozzi, Rozzi, I've heard that name before. London, Bond Street. I wonder if he's any relation to Mr Rozzi of Bond Street – ?" Then, laughing to Jenny, "I should say it would be long odds on it being so, all that happened in 1885! Not a racing cert!"

Jenny, intent on making up the two weeks that had been lost without Pimbo's motivation, came up with a nice little barber's story that she had filched from an old Journal; Pimbo excitedly read the story. 'Sevvy', as he was known, because of his love of Seville oranges, coupled with the fact, that during the First World war he had officiated as the Regimental barber, add to this the growing popularity of the comic opera 'The Barber of Seville', thus, he was always known as Sevvy. At the end of the 1914–1918 war Sevvy did a spell in India, as did a good many servicemen. It was here, that Sevvy cottoned on to the idea of becoming a travelling barber, many of whom could be seen in the streets of Cairo earning a living by giving instant haircuts or shaves on the crowded pavements. The Army had instilled into the barber a wanderlust, and the fear of unemployment, which was rife in those days, was the crowning factor that drove Sevvy into his new vocation.

A morning spent at Jim Lee's at the corner of River Lane, saw him fitted out by the little street-trader-supplied, with the required barbering equipment and a small case to hold everything. Sevvy had brought away with him from the Army as a memento of his sojourn as Regimental Barber, his favourite pair of hand-clippers and open-razor. Thus he was ready for the unusual trade of travelling barber. 'Have case, will travel' became Sevvy's maxim.

The next thing was to obtain a good strong carrier-bike, as Sevvy intended to travel from one village to another as cheaply as possible. The 'Old Man' Townsend, as he was known, supplied a new carrier for 5/- down and 2/6 thereafter, weekly. Sevvy left the little Norfolk Street cycle shop ready for anything!

Caldecote, a small village on the way to St

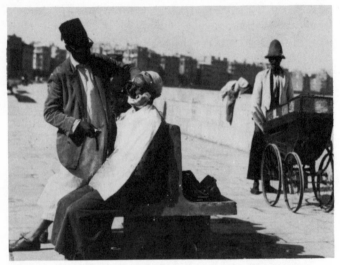

*The travelling barber on the streets of Cairo which incited
"Sevvy" on his adventures.*

Neots was known as Tin Town. It boasted very
little in the way of domestic amenities, so our
barbering hero decided to make it his first call.

As Sevvy looked down from a small hillock on to
the array of corrugated iron constructions, it reminded him of the scene from Charlie Chaplin's
Gold Rush, just a desolate waste waiting to be
explored. The barber's first call was at the one and
only shop in the village, that of a certain Mr
Sparks. It was little more than a tin atrocity, a
large sign outside on which was written 'Fresh
Fish Daily' was completely incongruous to the
whole set-up. The owner was a thin little man,
with spiked hair that Sevvy longed to get his

scissors into; he'd never before seen such uncontrolled spiky hair.

"What can I do you for, Sir?" asked Mr Sparkes in a squeeky voice, in harmony with the whole appearance. Sevvy, blinked. "I'm a travelling barber, good sir. A new venture, I might add, but, seeings as you folks in Caldecote don't seem to have much in the hairdressing line – well, I'm here with my equipment, rarin' to go!"

The shop owner grinned, as he ran his fingers through his unruly crop, "Well, I get it cut once a year. Ol' Boyce runs his shears over it for me, I keep a cap on for a few days after to let it settle, before I let's it all hang out!"

At that moment a small boy peeped his head around the door. To Sevvy's surprise he was a miniature copy of Mr Sparkes, hair just as unruly.

"Well, orlright, you can see what you can do with my boy 'Sonny' They set him home from school, because the kids laugh at him, and call him 'Carrot-top'. It ain't fair on him to keep him away from school for the lack of a haircut!"

Sonny was good as the barber sat him on a chair in the kitchen and trimmed away at his flowing unruly locks. Sevvy felt good; a job at his first call. By the time he finished, the barber reckoned the schoolkids and the teachers wouldn't know Sonny. Another thing, maybe the other kids would like theirs cut on similar lines. Sevvy had introduced the Boston Cut to the sleepy little village – Sonny confirmed his liking for the new style, "They won't laugh at me now, will they Sir?"

Back in the shop, Mr Sparkes was busily stacking a small crate of Sevvy's favourite oranges.

"What's the damage, Sir? Why bless my soul, he looks a real little dapper-dan?"

Sonny's dad looked on with admiration at the splendid transformation.

The barber smiled. "Three-pence to you Sir! Quite a lot to get off – and if you can throw in a couple of oranges, I'll call it square!"

Sevvy's next call was at a tiny bungalow, deep into a small patch of grass surrounded by a large orchard, on the gate in crumpled letters was the sign 'Rose Cottage'. The occupant, a dear little rosy cheeked old lady welcomed Sevvy into a small cosy room at the rear of the bungalow. "You'd have never got down here in the winter, up to your neck in mud it is. So you're a barber, eh? My dear hubby passed away a year ago, so's there no trade here for you – but, all the same have a cup of tea with me, I don't often get a visitor."

Over a cup of tea the old lady said, as how Caldicote one day would spread out. After the war, some with a bit of savings came out here from Cambridge; bought a pig or two, a few chickens, built up gradually, even built their own bungalow. Take Mr Boyce for instance, got a big spread now, large hen houses, sells eggs to the shops all round, even in Cambridge; they say this Christmas he'll be selling hundreds of fresh chickens for the oven. Same with pigs really, that fellow Fletcher built up a good business, you'd never know how, reckon they'll be doing pig studies at his styes afore long."

In the corner of the room, Sevvy spotted what he thought to be small dolls lying on a table close to the widow.

The widow smiled as she noticed his curiosity.

"They're corn-dollies, we use them at the Harvest Festival. We've only got about a dozen churchgoers in the village; we use the school-room at the top of the main road. We make a few pence on them, all helps to fill the collection plate!"

Picking one up Sevvy, taking out his scissors from his case, began cutting away at the top of the doll's full crop of wheat-stack hair. In next to no time, he'd fashioned out a beautiful halo resembling something akin to an Icon, with a background of splendour behind a lovely face.

"There!" he said, triumphantly holding it up to the astonished lady's gaze "'A Harvest Halo'. Should fetch a little bit more for the collection plate!"

Hurrying across to a drawer in the table she fished out an armful of other corn-dollies. "You've got a job here, after all, make these as you have that one and I'll pay you the price of two haircuts. The vicar will be as pleased as Punch, he can sell them to visitors at his Manse in Bourne"

Sevvy, of course obliged. Although he turned away the offer of the price of two haircuts, the widow insisted that he take the money. "The Lord didn't send you all this way for nothing!"

The barber's next call was in an area called Greenfields, here the bungalows seemed a little more impoverish than the others. At the end of some of the shacks, were amateurish attempts at building a kind of extension.

The reason for this Sevvy was soon to find out.

"If you're a tally-man, you can push off" shouted a wiry little woman hanging out washing the

colour of which induced the barber to think that
she'd been forcing grey in, instead of out.

"What's it you're after?" she added, as Sevvy
walked down a cinder-ash path leading to the
bungalow. The sound of squabbling children came
through an open window.

"I'm a travelling barber, ma'am. Maybe, in the
wilds of Tin Town as you called it, someone,
instead of trapsing into Cambridge, might want a
cut-and-trim, that goes for ladies as well –
ma'am!"

The washerwoman sat on an old tree stump and
viewed her visitor. She reckoned he must have
been an ex-servicman, trying to ferret out a world
fit for such as he to live in. She smiled to herself at
his tact of the 'Wilds of Tin Town' – didn't stop her
wastrel son's family from plonking themselves
down on her charity, and she with no husband at
that. Been thrown out Doric Street, they had, not
paying the rent her daughter-in-law had said.
Still smoked up to forty woodbines a day he did,
with three kids to keep and no job – too lazy to get
up in the morning. So he dumped his family on to
her. "Won't be for long, Mum. Soon as I can
straighten myself out!" he'd promised. She gave
him a little bit of ground to manage, get a few
vegetables grown for his family. After the first day
of digging he said his back went. He's done nothing but sit about listening to the radio.

Alice, her daughter-in-law, got a part-time job
with Mr Boyce the poulterer, collecting and cleaning eggs. It was only a stone's throw away from
the bungalow – at least it paid a bit for the extra
mouths to feed.

After her little day dream, the woman stood up. "I'm Brenda, you can have a cup of tea with me. Alice put in a little extra time at Boyce's. Her eldest boy could do with his hair trimmed, it's all over his eyes, Bobby's his name!"

As the day was fine and warm, Brenda spared the barber a look into the condition of the inside of the shack, by bringing out two chairs, one for Sevvy and one for the boy customer. The tea went down well, and the boy chatted away as the barber got to work.

"What do you want to be when you grow up?" ventured Sevvy.

Bobby blinked "There's nothing round here, mum says!" The piggeries are spoke for, anyway, you have to pay a premium to learn all about pigs, it's different now. When I'm fourteen, next year, I'm going to buy a bike and work as an errand boy in Cambridge. The Whippet bus goes into town every morning, and back at 6 pm – but it's 1/6 each way, it would take all my wage, I wouldn't be able to give mum anything!"

Sevvy admired the boy. It was about 12 miles into Cambridge, on the return journey, he would catch the Madingley hill to climb. Maybe on a windy day he would have to walk up the very steep incline. They said in the village that Sparkes did the journey twice a week to collect his fresh fish. He reckoned the old fellow had guts, and on an old trade bike, too!

Alice gave Sevvy 2^d at the end of his stint. But, pulling out an egg from her apron pocket, she offered it boiled, with a slice of bread, as the motivation to cut yet another kid's hair.

"I picks up a rogue egg here and there. You know, it gets laid in places outside the hen-house. Boycey don't mind, he's a good sort and he knows how I'm placed!"

After leaving the house, the barber checked up on his takings so far. He'd picked up several snacks on his visits, which of course saved him a bit of cash. His cash flow was now up to £5 and he'd two more days to go for the week to be up. True, £1 of this, was for doing a bit of lifting for a well-to-do fruit grower in the village, but Sevvy was satisfied. The going wage in Cambridge was around £3–£4 a week, that is, if you could get a job.

The post-war days had certainly bred a batch of go-getters. There were travelling scissor-grinders, mat-repairers, umbrella men, organ-grinders, buskers, odd-job men, and now the likes of himself.

One day maybe, should he save enough, he might be able to rent a little shop. After all, he'd no one to keep but himself. Not the marrying sort was Sevvy, he'd seen enough double-crossing during his Army days – but who knows, should the right one come along?

In the centre of Caldecote were a string of houses in the course of erection. He reckoned one day the place might grow; down would come the old tin shacks. Already, Sevvy had seen building sites marked out beside the little bungalows. As the inhabitants prospered, fruitgrowing, pigs, vegetables and even live-stock, Caldecote would have its first Post Office, and a regular bus service instead of having to walk to the main road. Mr

Boyce, already, had strengthened his lay-out to twice its original size. He had fitted the hen-houses out with special lighting and had installed automatic drink dispensers, a little van proudly bore his name.

E. Boyce
Poulterer. Live chicks
Fresh eggs

The barber's last call in Caldecote, was to a dear old man called Humpty. A little dwarf-like man, his nickname appropriate to his appearance. Humpty lived alone in a tiny hut-like contraption at the end of a small wood. Amazingly, he was a writer who specialised in little tales of woodland creatures. He would send off his snippets to various periodicals, complete with a photograph of his little subjects.

Humpty readily allowed Sevvy to cut and trim his small beard and also to cut his bushy overflowing hair.

"Couldn't live in a better place, right on top of my work!" he grinned as Sevvy hacked away. "Went to Canada when things were bad. Picked up a bit of money as a trapper. Now, here I am, doing what I like best and getting paid for it!"

"I suppose one day, this little bit of paradise will be cut down to make way for more houses. Guess, I'll go with it when it does get the chop!"

After a cup of coffee, Humpty slipped a pound-note into Sevvy's hand. "There you are! You're doing a good job. One day you'll make it good, like I did, make no mistake, boy, you'll make it good!"

The barber rode away on his trade-bike into the nearby village of Bourne, with a distant view of old Humpty's "To make it good!"

Sevvy, during a visit to a small village known as Dry Drayton, picked up rather an unusual customer. He was a little man, almost bursting out from a Walt Disney cartoon. Carrying a sack over his shoulder from which seemed to be forthcoming a hissing, grunting and groaning noise, followed by a series of in-and-out bulging contortions, giving the sack the appearance of having inside, a host of mischievous gremlins.

"I'm Jimmy Lupman" said the little stranger. Sevvy eyed him up and down from the top of his woolly type skull cap, down through the quaint weather-proof jacket, to his wellies with coloured football stockings peeping from their turned-down tops.

"I've heard about your travelling salon. I need a haircut and trim; the early morning mists are getting at my beard and side-burns. Trouble is, I'm not getting any younger but I've still got to pay the rent and rates!"

"What's your game, then?" asked Sevvy, a little concerned about the goings-on inside the sack.

Jimmy laughed, "Ah, they all ask that! I'm the local poacher-cum-animal research worker. I work for the Animal Research Laboratory. At the moment I'm gathering in a harvest of frogs and toads; this time of the year they spawn. I suppose you noticed the sign down the road 'Toads and Frogs Crossing the Road. Motorists Beware!' The Lab pays me well, at the same time I keep my eyes open for a stray pheasant or two"

The travelling barber smiled as he finished off Jimmy's previously wild beard. Madingly and Dry Drayton, nestling close together, were real go-getters in the village world of East Anglia!

CHAPTER 17

Sarah's Poem

Jenny was still putting in strenous efforts to ascertain the new project would cover every aspect of hairdressing, this time she had uncovered a glossy magazine's glowing account as to the reason why barber's and ladies' hairdressing salons are equivalent to an expensive visit to a psychologist.

Most hairdressers are, in their own right, amateur psychotherapists. One famous salon keeper calls the service he gives to women trichotherapy. He gave an example of his service to a reporter at his deluxe West End salon. "We look and listen and ask what our clients want, if you have a giving nature you can talk to anyone." He went on, "The fact that my father was a psychotherapist, gave me a thought that when you work with people you don't just look at their hair."

Staring at me at eye level, he said "You're not just looking at my reflection. You make eye contact, not to intimidate them, but to show that you care about them. My job is not to develop in them a false image potential – but to help them feel good about themselves.

"It's because customers know that they can trust us and that we are on their side. If they say they want to look like Nazimova, all hair and allure, we won't snigger, but will search for their natural image potential.

"We haven't got an 'O' level between us in this salon, but we all know how to build up a relationship with a client. Not just for a quick buck, but for our reputation to give satisfaction!

"Sometimes it backfires! Once you've taken someone who is depressed and into themselves and got them feeling good again, and looking good, they sometimes stop coming because they don't want you to remember them when they were down and unhappy.

"Should a client mention to you about suspected infidelity of their husband, you don't go into too intimate conclusions, you ask what would they do should they find it to be true?

"Tending clients hair in readiness for the funeral of their spouse, or actually servicing an adulterous triangle, can be depressing. But it's the reciprocation that stops him being the rubbish bin for emotional trauma.

"'You've got a very long face, so if we bailed your hair up it won't look so slim, and I can reduce your highlight'. This gives a client confidence in me. Every customer gets an idea of what we can do, this is the start of building up a lasting customer-relationship. He paused, then went on "They give you an account of what is happening to them, their marriage, their job. Then I talk about my children, and our bond is established, we can do business together.

"It's not a sexual relationship, it's sensual. It's better than a friend-girl friend relationship because sometimes this can end in bitterness, but that doesn't apply in our case. I'm married but I do get customers, occasionally, who act as though I'm not. One lady showed me raunchy snaps of herself, but I'm too far in love to be interested.

"I work on the principle that customers, having confided in you secrets they would not have told their partners, bosses, doctors, or bank managers, trot out happy in the knowledge that they have been relieved of a burden; and that it will travel no further than the ears of the person, snipping around their's."

The journal also showed snippets to support the narrative of the former famous salon, by actually visting and servicing a woman who had lost an adulterous husband, which had caused her a stay inside a mental clinic. "I made her look beautiful, and lent a sympathetic ear which finally boosted her confidence, allowing her to leave the clinic" he pointed out.

"Another hairdressing therapist made short shrift with advice to a client whose boyfriend was two-timing her. When she called his home she got just an answering machine. Our hero advised her to change her name, get the secretary to put her through, and then challenge him on his behaviour – she obtained satisfactory results!

"Another client was in tears as she told of her

husband's cruelty in battering her about. 'I told her to get out, leave him!' said the hairstylist. 'She did just that and we've been friends ever since!'

"One client, as her hair was being shampooed, burst into uncontrollable tears. We sat her down and she poured out her heart. This, in one of London's most fashionable salons. It turned out that her husband had just left her!

"A gentleman's barber confessed. 'I've had many male clients over the years, who were happily married, but were really gay. They would often ask my advice.'

"Many well known entertainers in show business, accept that the price of a hairdo or snip, as they rinse out their problems with their hairdresser, is much cheaper and sometimes more beneficial, than a visit to an expensive psychologist."

The magazine article ended in what hairdressers say – but, what they really mean:

● Have you been on holiday yet? *they mean* I can't think of anything else to say

● How's work? *they mean* I can't remember what you do

● Are you going out tonight? *they mean* If not, you're very boring

● You've got a good crop of hair! *they mean* My, what a mess

● Where did you last have it cut? *they mean* Was

it a basin cut?

● Have you ever thought of growing your hair? *they mean* It's far too short

● Would you like a conditioner? *they mean* That will be an extra £1.50 please

Pimbo, was well pleased with Jenny's effort. It confirmed the fact that hairdressers were a real pillar of society and, as more ladies' salons were opening up all over the country, changes all round in terms of technique and home spun advice, by mature hairstyling men and women, would safeguard the domestic issues for the coming generations.

Jenny wasn't finished with her side of the project, to her boyfriend's surprise she drew from her pocket a slip of note paper on which was written a poem. It was from Sarah Thomas, an eleven year old schoolgirl, with an address at 27 Perse Way. A short note, preceding the poem ran: Dear Jenny, all the girls at school know about what you and Pimbo are doing by writing about barbers and lady hairdressers. As I recently won a poetry competition, they dared me to write a poem and send it to you. Love Sarah. P.S. I hope you both like it. Pimbo read as follows:

'Snippetty-Snap'

The scissors go snap,
Hair floats to your lap.
Short, long, brown, or black,

Most of your hair, you now will lack.

You might lose an ear,
But, won't lose a tear,
Because, if you hate long hair
Just sit in the barber's chair.

Don't be late on the very first date,
Otherwise, you'll get more than a 'crop'
It's worse than the Dentist,
It's as bad as the Chemist.
You see, I'm going to the Barber's shop!!

Everyone, hates it, when it comes to the fringe,
Whenever he cuts it, I shudder and cringe.
I'm shaking all over–
How I wish it were over!

The hot steamy towel, whipped round your face,
I can assure you, it's not made of *lace*.
You'll feel fresh as the rain
When, you're next, at the Barber's again!

Getting rid of the spikes upon your chin,
Feeling the blade, as sharp as a Dolphin's fin.
Your hair is fluffy, just like fur,
Would you like Brylcream – Sir?

Pimbo laughed as he finished reading the delightful little snippet of child's poetry. He wondered at Sarah's command of imagery at such a tender age. He felt that she had conjured up a very good vision of a barber's establishment. He pointed out the genuine little pangs of fear that the girl had hinted at. Jenny, reckoned it was because of the old tales and customs of the barber's shop.

"Worse than the dentist?" Maybe Sarah had seen the film of 'Sweeny Todd' the demon barber, to a small child would, indeed, be worse than the Dentist.

"As bad as the chemist? might this allude to the nasty tasting potions that chemist supplies. The thought of blood-sucking leeches, might well have turned the tide against the poor old barber!"

Then again, a young lady's fear of losing the fringe which, during her early years, had protected her from being too responsible for a few temper tantrums. Now, as Mummy would say "You're getting too grown up for that kind of behaviour Sarah!."

But Pimbo loved the hot towel part of the poem. He wondered how Sarah had learned about such things as hot towels,. Perhaps through a Chaplin or W.C. Fields comedy at the flicks 'Fresh as the rain', what a lovely thought. Pimbo reckoned that as soon as he were old enough he'd get Albert Scott to give him a sample of how a hot towel really felt – fresh as the rain!

Then again 'the spikes on you chin'! Pimbo, had seen many, on the chins of the old men awaiting service on Sunday morings, outside Phil Holmes place on East Road.

The old cut-throat, 'as sharp as a Dolphin's fin', no wonder a little fear had crept into Sarah's lovely little set of verses. But, it all ended so well!

'Hair as fluffy as fur – would you prefer Brylcream, Sir?'

The old pawnbroker of Fitzroy Street.

The two young friends sat together on a seat overlooking Parker's Piece. After the poem reading and its analysis, they felt like a break away from the barber's chain. But somehow it wasn't to be; Fred Rule, the veteran custodian, was giving the green sward a once over in readiness for the spate of weekend cricket matches.

The lawn mower was cutting a lovely pattern around the existing wicket. Pimbo could visualise Scotty's clippers running up and down someone's hair. As though that wasn't enough, one of the groundsman, Bill, was trimming the edges of the

pitch with something approaching the likes of a
cut-throat razor.

Further down, a water sprinkler was at work
gently spraying one side of the wicket. This, to
Pimbo, represented a shampoo. Jenny laughed, it
seemed that she, too, had been thinking on similar lines to those of her boyfriend.

"Oh, well! It's our own fault, we've let it get into
our system. Miss Franklin, at art class, said we
must get right into the skin of our part, that way
we'll produce something more realistic!"

At Jenny's words, Pimbo nodded. He wanted
the project to be good. If Sarah could write about a
barber's shop, and she a girl, too, well then they
ought, with two heads placed together, write
something worthwhile for the next generation to
enjoy.

Fred Rule, shouting across to one of the
groundsmen broke Pimbo's thoughts.

"I might be a bit late back from dinner, Bill, the
missus says I need a haircut. Scotty will let me in
during the dinner hour!"

At this, Pimbo gave up completely!!

CHAPTER 18

Sevvy Continues as Travelling Barber

With the weather on his side, Sevvy found himself travelling much further than he at first planned. Having done the village of Bourne, with quite excellent results our hero found himself at a small village called Bushmead, on the outskirts of Bedford. It seemed to have got its name from the amount of market gardeners living in its confines, and with its plentiful supply of various shrubs on sale.

The village, although small, was rather widely spread and Sevvy soon picked himself out a nice little thatched cottage for his first call. The old chap who answered Sevvy's knock, must have been near the 80 mark. He'd managed to reach the door on two sticks, but sank immediately into a nearby chair, which apparently was there to cushion any likely fall. His face was ruddy and healthy looking, befitting a man of the soil.

"What's it you want? You look a decent sort,

better come in than stand outside. If you pinched everything I've got, it wouldn't amount to much"

The old man hobbled across to his favourite hearthside chair, leaving the barber to take over the one he'd just vacated.

"I'm old Ted Jakes, lived on my own for the last ten years since me missus died. Hardly ever gets a visitor, except the postmistresses, who slips in with me pension once a week. I shaves meself when I feels like it, but if you like you can trim me beard, the tobacco plays hell with the bottom of it – goes all brown like!"

Sevvy went to work on the old fellow, and for an extra bonus, trimmed around his ears and neck.

As he finished old Ted off, he wondered how much to charge. He would have liked to have thrown it all in free, but after all, if he once started it, everyone would be jumping on the band-waggon. Ted helped him out. "Tell you what, boy, you can do another bit of cut and trim for me. I haven't been up the cemetery for two or three years it's me missus grave. I've only got a daughter and she's took off to Canada. I don't like to ask anyone in the village, they're all busy working. What do you say? I'll give you a 1/- to cover the lot"

On the barber's agreement, the old chap pencilled down a description of his wife's resting place. "You can't miss it, it's right up the corner, near the stand-pipe!"

Sevvy found the site quite easily, mainly because as Bushmead was the home of market gardeners, most of the graves had been carefully tended, many with expensive marble headstones surrounded by evergreen shrubs. Ted's wife had

very little in the way of embellishment no headstone or surround, it was just a grassy mound,
easily recognised as a former grave. A rusting,
black, cast-iron cross with the discernible name of
'Dora' was stuck forcibly in the centre of the
mound, as though to have put it in as a headstone,
might well have resulted in losing the site forever.

The cast-iron cross, was about 18 inches long,
and nine inches wide. Sevvy had seen many
before, they were widely used by the poor, at
poor-law funerals; and paupers, at various work-
houses, were buried beneath such symbols. The
cross, sold at funeral parlours, stone masons and
ironmongers, was guaranteed for five years, at the
price of 1/6^d.

Sevvy reckoned that this cross had about one
year to go. In the distance, the barber spotted
a small hut of the kind, at cemeteries, where
mourners collect watering cans and deposit empty
flower cartons or pots; maybe borrow a tool of
some description in order to carry out a refurbish-
ment.

A farm labouring type of chap, was busily
tidying up the place. At the sight of the barber, he
thrust out a soil stained palm. "I'm the cemetry
odd job man. Keep the place as spruce as possible.
Kind of voluntary, £52 annual fee, summer or
winter. Bob's me name! Works out at £1 a week."

The barber smiled, he reckoned that Bob hadn't
done a pounds worth of work on Dora's grave for
many a year. The odd job man must have read his
mind. "I see you pottering around old Ted's missus' grave, she was a good un, pity Ted spoilt it
all."

"You mean?" queried Sevvy.

"I have orders not to touch the grave, no one dare! The parish Councillor, he's dead now, used to be a big farmer round this area. Ted was his cowman. Then came the big strike. Labourers were fighting for a living wage after the farmers had actually docked down their former wage. Bushmead was lucky, most of them were market gardeners, the strike didn't effect them as much as the farmers." Bob paused, then went on.

"Gradually, the farm workers went back. But, Ted Jakes held out. I reckon as cowman, he put in a lot longer hours than the farm workers, at calving, and weekends, and early morning milking, you know what it is"

The councillor-cum-farmer, never forgave Ted for that.

"So the village sent poor old Ted to Coventry – is that it?" asked Sevvy.

Bob nodded. "The Councillor practically ruled the village in those days. Whereas, I had been given a freehand at tending the graves, on Ted's wife's death I had orders from him to keep away from the site"

"But surely you could show a little goodwill, especially now the Councillor has passed away?" asked Sevvy

"Not so! My wife gets on at me. Threatens to come down and do it herself, she and Dora were good pals. You see–" added Bob, a trifle ruefully "I'm farm foreman; the Councillor's son has taken over the farm and it'd be more than my job's worth. But I'll tell you this. Next year I'm on retirement and Dora's grave will look as good as anyone's when I've finished with it. I owe it to poor old Ted, whose too infirm to get down here."

The barber was pleased at Bob's promise. "I see you have some shears around here. Care to give me loan of them so's I can get the grave ship-shape, until you get at it next year?"

Bob dutifully obliged, also lending Sevvy a small digging fork and trowel. Nodding his head towards a small clump of plants and shrubbery, he winked saucily.

"Help yourself. I'm off to the farm, I've seen nothing, and nobody!"

Sevvy did a good job on the grave and its surrounds.

In the hut he found a thrown away globe with an interior of artificial flowers. It was very popular in those days. Maybe the owner had thought it old fashioned and plumped for the new type of flower container. The barber wiped it clean under the stand-pipe, and found it almost intact, with the exception of a few minor scratches.

The cast-iron cross was certainly on its last legs. But Sevvy polished it up as best he could. Sticking plaster, which he might have used on a client's cut chin, he placed over the top of clumped newspaper, making the worn part of the cross into a kind of papier-mâché, this he mullified with gelatine which, of course, was the poorman's brilliantine.

The barber smiled as he surveyed his handi-work. He'd used many of his working tools, even scissors for clipping along the awkward parts of the grave and for shortening the stalks of the flowers that Bob had kindly given him.

He reckoned that old Ted would be well pleased. Then it dawned on him that the old boy wouldn't be able to see the newly touched-up grave of his missus. In his case, Sevvy carried a small camera, a Brownie they were usually known as. He carefully checked the camera for film and adjustment, then standing a small distance away, with the sunlight in perfect position for a snap-shot, Sevvy took a picture of the grave. The glass bowl, standing out well in the centre of the mound, Sevvy was sure, would catch the eye of the old husband.

As he finished, Bob suddenly appeared. "Left me jacket behind" he said, picking up an old working jacket from the rear of the shed. "Comes in handy when I'm doing a dirty job – hullo, my, you've made a difference to the grave area – taken a snap as well I see?"

The barber explained about the idea of old Ted, not being ambulent enough to get down to the cemetery, so perhaps a snap shot would do the trick.

"Been talking to the missus, mate. Told her about you; we both realised that all this nonsense had gone far enough. Poor Old Dora wouldn't have thought much of the goings on. Tell you now mate, after I gets aways from the farm, I'll see that old Ted gets to see his missus' grave even if I have to carry him on my back!"

Bob was watching Sevvy about to put the Brownie back into his case. "Reckon you'd best give me the film, boy. You'll be long gone, time the post-office get the photo back. I'll see Ted gets it, he'll have something to look at for the rest of his days!"

The barber handed over the film. He'd planned somehow to get back to the village and collect it – but Bob had saved him the worry and time. The farm foreman wasn't finished.

"What's more, the wife's invited you back home for supper – you can kip down for the night, then leave in the morning. The next village is some twelve miles away. Another thing, I can do with a haircut, and she needs a trim – how's about it?"

Sevvy, of course, was delighted to accept all three offers!

As Autumn approached, Sevvy decided to get back into the warmth of the City. He had done everything that he wanted to. Economy-wise, he'd more than paid his way. True at times, he'd wandered away from the professional side of hair-dressing by taking on such jobs as poor old Jake's, it was a good thing that no one had snitched on him to the Hairdressers Federation, but, most of those jobs had led back to a hairdressing tack. On top of that, a square meal and a warm bed plus, at times, a few of his favourite Seville oranges.

Then too, over the months he'd stashed away his cycle money at 2/6 per week, he'd have to see old Townsend and get his credit card up to date. So it was, that the travelling barber entered Norfolk Street, and thus into Townsend's cycle shop.

Sevvy smiled as he looked up at the penny-farthing cycle, which the cycle dealer had hanging on the wall of his shop. He reckoned it would have been a very rough ride over some of the places he had ridden of late.

Mr Townsend greeted him warmly. "Reckon I

was just about thinking of sending the van after you to collect the bike, but they told me you were going round the sticks shaving the country yokels. I fathomed you'd be earning enough to pay the installments!"

The barber paid his dues, the veteran cycle dealer stamped his card to date. "I'm thinking of retiring, Sevvy. My son Chris, will be taking over. There's talk that all the little shops along here will be going; Masons, the chemist, Goode the sweet-shop, and the little greengrocer chappie – I reckon it'll land us! into Burleigh Street!"

Few people realise, that barber's themselves need haircuts. Sevvy, during his session away had accumulated a heavy crop so decided to allow Twinkle-Toes-Harrison to do the job of transforming his locks into a presentable feature of his face. Mr Harrison's lightness on his feet, his dancing ability, plus the fact that he was a fine pianist and ran a dance band of his own, gave him the most apt name of Twinkle-toes, but it could easily have been twinkle-fingers as well!

As he was snipping away at his peer's hair, he seemed a little more concerned than usual. Sevvy tackled him on the reason for his mood that morning.

"It's the Beacky" he answered. "Seems though they may not get their licence renewed. Residents around the area have been complaining of the noise. Motor bike revving, car door slamming, raucous laughter as club members leave the hall. I get a good number of gigs there, seems I shall have to search for a new venue!"

Sevvy nodded. The Beaconsfield Hall had been

one of the really famous dance halls in Cambridge situated in Gwydir Street it had given easy access to the residents of that area. He reckoned that new generations were now using the hall, coming in from the villages at weekends with noisy motor bikes. Things had changed so quickly, from the sedate little tea-dances, with the local dancing expert, Mr Curwain, teaching the steps; to the beer-swilling antics of a minority, who were making it bad for those wanting nothing more than an entertaining dancing session.

Twinkle-toes went on. "Seems that it all depends on a chap called Murfett who has a big say concerning entertainment rules of the Town. Worked his way up from ordinary working class, they tell me. He's in the running for the big-wig presiding over the Magistrates Court. Nice chap, likes to see social justice done; he's interested in choral events, too. I'm sure he'll be fair, but the trouble is that the noise is getting a bit out of hand for the elderly to stomach – this fellow Murfett's sure to be on their side!

After his lengthy tirade, the kindly barber paused as he held the mirror at the back of Sevvy's head. "O.K? I know you'll O.K. any of my work. They tell me your'e staying in Cambridge for the winter, now I've got a proposition for you. I'm having a long break, taking a month off, I reckon this Beaconsfield Hall lark has got me down. I'd like you to act as locum, stand-in for me you can use the spare room at the back for living quarters – and of course use of the kitchen and domestic facilities – are you on?"

Sevvy nearly fell out of the chair in his excitement to say 'Yes'. Mr Harrison wasn't finished handing out goodies. "As a member of the Hairdresser's Association, I'm in touch with most of the barbers in Cambridge. I can get you enough stand-in jobs to last you all winter – and summer too, if you want"

Thus it was that our hero, ended his 'have case, will travel' days and settled down, met a nice little lady friend, married her. After three years as a locum, he took over a little shop of his own, next door to a shop that stocked Seville oranges!!

C. Lanham's shop in King Street.

CHAPTER 19

Len Tibbs
(Barber Extraordinaire)

Pimbo's next barber for research was a most extroverted character, in that he was also a great name in the entertainment world. He ran his own dance band, arranged concert parties, and had the distinction of playing for six weeks at the famous Windmill Theatre in London's square mile. Len Tibbs' exploits in show business are, of course, subject for a separate novel, we will deal with his barbering adventures.

Len began as an apprentice with Mr H.E. Kent of 64 Cherryhinton Road. Len's dad, during the dark days of the unemployment, insisted that his son must learn a trade. With no real motive of becoming a barber the boy, Len, went down to the Local Labour Exchange to find out what there was going in the apprenticeship line – it was either that, or errand-boy. The only thing in, at the time, was the request for an apprentice by Mr H.E. Kent, whose private residence was that of Blinco

Grove, with his barbering establishment at 64 Cherry Hinton Road.

The master-barber turned out to be a very hard taskmaster and kept Len hard at it from 8 am until 7 pm. Among Len's duties was the cleaning out of a large copper urn, which was used for the hot water supply. Now and again (a fault in copper), it would turn a nasty green colour, which, meant using a special acid solution.

Poor young Len hated this task, it made him cough and sneeze and sometimes almost faint.

Len's pay was of the increment variety 3/6 per week the first year, 4/6 per week the second, rising to the ultimate of 5/- at the end of the third year.

The young apprentice, at one time experienced a part of his master's suspicious nature. It was Len's duty to pay the weekly paper bill at a newsagent's shop a few yards from the barber's shop. It seemed tht the girl responsible for booking in the money had been 'dipping her fingers' in the till.

To Mr Kent's surprise, a bill for the monies he'd sent with his apprentice, was sent to him, along with a curt request for payment. It was some time before the matter was settled, with Len's innocence confirmed – but the young boy never felt the same respect for his master after the incident.

Len told Pimbo of his first shaving of a customer. At Mr Kent's request "Would you mind my apprentice trying out his first time shave on you?" a customer obliged.

Len confessed how nervous he was, and promptly proceeded to cut lumps out of the customer's cheek.

In those days, the boy lived in Thoday Street, and remembers walking home from the shop through Coleridge Road which, at the time was being actually constructed from an almost country lane aspect.

In time, his dad managed to obtain a bicycle for him, and wearing a new overcoat, Len caught the bottom of the coat in the forks of his front wheel, tipping him over the handle-bars. Len related to Pimbo a nice little ancedote that happened in the shop. It was a busy morning, and a small boy sat patiently waiting his turn Within just two customers of it being his turn, the boy suddenly rose and hurriedly left the shop. This caused a speculation among Len's customers as to why the boy, after waiting so long, had left the shop.

Within minutes, the boy was back again, but of course had lost his place in the queue.

Len couldn't resist asking the boy why he'd gone from the shop in the first place.

To everyone's merriment, the boy replied "I went down to George Bendall's the other barber's down the road – but he was just as busy as you!"

The customers were so taken back with the boy's sheer innocence they allowed him to take the next turn!

After serving his three years under Mr Kent, Len moved on to a Mr Harleck of 78 Regent Street. At that time, Percy Reed, (the well known master-barber of later years) was working as an improver, a status that Len had now reached at an improved wage of 7/6 to start, rising to 12/6 when established.

One of Len's customers at the time was Tom Hayward, the well known cricketer and bosom pal of Jack Hobbs. Tom was often in a merry condition by the time he reached the shop; Len reckoned he'd probably scored a century! Mr Harleck, was a keen musician and had two lovely daughters, who kept an exclusive scent shop in Post Office Terrace, close by Muspratt's the famous photographers.

Sad to relate, Mr Harleck's wife suffered from senile-dementia, which caused her to walk into the shop during busy sessions inquiring blankly, in a loud voice, such like things as "I can't find the saucepan" or, "where'd you put the sauce bottle?"

This eccentric behaviour was too much for the master-barber, who gradually wound up his business.

Len, sensing the end, had given a week's notice, taking up an appointment with Mr Jolly of 25 St Andrew's Street.

Among his new employer's many customers, was the yet to be, Lord Cockcroft, the man responsible for much research into the splitting of the atom. On that wonderful occasion, Lord Cockcroft came into the shop crying out, "We've done, we've done it!"

It was here under Mr Jolley that Len was taught ladies hair trimming.

Several artistes from the adjacent New Theatre, were among Len's customers; one being the illustrious Louis Armstrong. The great man had a very tough upper lip, almost a kind of ridge. He would never allow Len to touch this part of his features. Louis, would take the razor from Len,

A snapshot from Mr Jolley's barber shop in St Andrews Street, 1920s (where Len Tibbs worked).

then after carefully trimming the required spot, hand it back with the words "Son, ah jest daren't chance it, I'd never be able to blow mah trumpet agin!"

Len had many a quaint smile at the college professors. Brilliant in brain, but entirely helpless with practical matters. Egg stains littered their ties and waistcoats, and when being brushed down, clouds of dust would spurt out from fading overcoats – just as a settee in the Munsters' films.

One well known pianist from the New Theatre, a certain Mr Aldeson, seemed to take a shine to our Len. When seated in the theatre watching a show, Len was put to the embarrassment of having Aldeson wave to him between piano lulls.

Another great character and a customer of the shop, was Mr Gray, of the partnership firm of estate agents Gray, Cook and Sons.

Mr Gray was always in a hurry! He would take great rapid strides to the barber's chair, then announce crisply "Shave!" and not utter another word during the service.

So much in a hurry was our Mr Gray, to avoid having to stop, he paid his bill weekly.

Len's next move was one of surprise. He moved back into his original shop at 64 Cherry Hinton Road. Mr Kent, his old boss had had enough, and was asking £250 for the goodwill of the shop. The building was on lease from the Rathmore Club, a few yards away.

Len signed himself up for the rentage of £10 per month, with a room above the shop to be under his jurisdiction.

It was then, to Len's utter astonishment, that one morning who should turn up for a shave but Mr Gray of Gray, Cook and Sons.

With his usually rapidity, Mr Gray took the chair, to ask curtly "What you doing here, then?"

At Len's explanation, he snapped "How much you paying?"

After Len had told, he snapped "I can help you!"

At the end of the week, when the barber went to his bank, Lloyd's at the corner of Rock Road, he found that Mr Gray had deposited exactly £250 in

Len's account. Len paid off the goodwill price of the shop, and instead of having to pay Mr Kent £10 monthly, was able to pay off Mr Gray's kind loan, at £5 per month.

Sadly, Mr Gray, ever in a hurry, whilst on the golf course had just urged his partner on with "Well, come on then!" when he collapsed and died.

Just as Len had settled all his debt regarding the shop – the war came. The now master-barber's new assistant Ken Knights, and a very able Ron Willis, looked after the shop in Len's absence at war.

Len vowed on joining up "Sod it, I can't cut hair in Civvy Street, so I won't cut hair in the Army!"

But he did take with him his barber's equipment, and artfully 'looked after' a few officers' hairdressing needs.

This obtained for Len, a little respite from square-bashing activities, and it was then his latent talent as an entertainer came to the fore. One of his army pals at the time, was the 'On the Buses' star, Reg Varney. With Reg, Len set up a good partnership playing the piano with Reg as vocal. The pair eventually took over the entertainment for the entire Division.

On coming back from the war, Len got further into the entertaining business. His dance band got under way, and during this time, he found out the loyal qualities of his partners at there shop, Ron Willis, and Len's wife Irene, who kept a wary eye on his purse strings, and curbed his tendency to overspend.

Pimbo asked Len about the earnings of barbers, which reputedly were given as high. This, the

master-man refuted. "Some days if you took £2 –
you were doing well!"

At 63 years, Len found that the lease on his
shop had expired, which meant that the Rathmore Club reluctantly had to double the rent.
With his dance band and other entertainments
giving him extra revenue, Len decided to call it a
day. He let the remainder of the lease at £10 per
month to a Mr Kingsly of Sawston.

Len had been at the shop for 40 years.

The barber, however, never left the trade completely. A room in Brooklands Avenue was
assigned him, where for two years he was chief
hairdresser to the team of Civil servants.

After a lot of conniving as to which room he
could use, Len felt this was a polite way of
terminating his engagement, so the barber got in
first, and left!

Len, still with an eye to boosting up his dance
band and entertaining revenue, took a job with
the Swiss Laundry in their carpet cleaning department. This he kept up until reaching pension-
able age.

With the oncoming years, he packed up his
dance band and with old adage ringing in his ears
'the show must go on' took up for 3–4 years, the
onerous task of being a Punch and Judy man his
wife Irene (bless her) helping out.

Len did local turns around the City.

Pimbo asked Len, which came first the barber
shop or his entertaining talent. After all, Len had
appeared on T.V. and had six glowing weeks at
the Windmill Theatre. He was the artiste who had
invented the character of the Railway Porter,

which had a regular turn on radio. He had given scores of regular concert appearances, and was once billed at the Windmill Theatre as 'The man who made them laugh – more than anyone!'

Len replied, a trifle ruefully "I had to think of my family, I didn't know how long my fame might last. I would loved to have entertained full time, and also Ron Willis was such a loyal chap to me when I was away on gigs – I wanted to keep him going at the shop!"

Thus it was, that dear old Len (now over 80) retired from active scenes of 'You're next Sir' and 'Your cue, Len – you're on now!'

Good luck Len and Irene on your retirement!!

CHAPTER 20

In Conclusion

Following Sarah Thomas's delightful poem on barbers, Pimbo was sent yet another by Natalie Manning, a young girl of 11 years. It seemed that Pimbo and Jenny's research into barber shops of old Cambridge had a similar reaction to that of the Pied Piper of Hamelin – poems, in lieu of rats! Natalie's contribution ran as follows:

Barbers cut our hair,
They cut it very well.
They cut from young to old,
The cowards *and* the bold.
They trim the famous and the rich,
Not to mention poor.
Just to name a few of those,
Would take for evermore.

They toil from morn, 'til night,
Their styles are most alluring,
They have little time for the outside world,
And oblige with manicuring.

Barbers work so hard, altering our mane,
Alas, to see it all a mess, when, caught out in the rain.
But, of course, without our barbers,
Our hair, we'd never train!

Natalie Manning (Aged 11 years)
39 Fox Hollow
Bar Hill
Cambridge

After reading the poem, Pimbo and Jenny realised what a lot of hidden talent there seemed to be, especially from youngsters like themselves.

At school next morning, Pimbo showed the work from both Sarah and Natalie to their art teacher, appropriately named Miss English.

The teacher spent the next lesson acquainting the class with ritual in Japan, where they celebrate their land, people and custom in what is known as Haiku. The Japanese are past masters in the art of miniaturization – capturing a delicate picture in a few words, using just 17 syllables. Amazingly, it was a Japanese barber, who first started the craze!

Haiku is a lesson in brevity. Each Haiku contains the name of a season or word to convey the time of the year. Snow, makes one think of Winter, Blossoms, calls out Spring, and Heat, a blazing Summer day.

The teacher gave the class a few examples.
A fallen petal
Flies back to its branch:
Ah! a butterfly!

Snail, my little man
Slowly, ah, very slowly
Climb up Mount Fuji

Just imagine the scene. Towering over 12,000 feet above sea level, Mount Fuji rises abruptly. To reach her top is no mean feat, but puny man must climb like a snail, ever so slowly. You can almost feel the aching limbs. Haiku is sometimes called the poetry of sensation, making the reader feel the setting.

Miss English, pointed out to the class, that Pimbo and Jenny's search into the barbers' history had woken up a latent desire for the two young girls to express their thoughts in poetry. Albeit, not quite as brief as that of the Japanese children, but never the less a stab into creative writing.

Jenny seemed a little worried as to whether or not all this had anything to do with the barber shop project. Pimbo eased her conscience by pointing out that had it not been for the project the two little girls would not have written their poems. Also, they too would never have been introduced to the lovely form of Haiku writing. Miss English was setting up a competition amongst the whole school, to find the best snippets of Haiku. It might even spread to other schools, and who knows, Cambridge might well be inundated with such creative art.

Jenny smiled, then nudged her boyfriend "What about you then? Write one yourself with a barber shop theme. See what you can do, then I'll have a go."

Pimbo drew from his pocket a slip of paper. "I've beaten you to it, Jenny. I had similar thoughts to yours, then realised that if I could manage one, I might follow up with more. We could get the school workshop to print them then take them round to all the barbers' still going strong and sell them for a few pence? He read to Jenny his first attempt at writing an Haiku, it ran:

Harvest field stubble

Akin to 7 o'clock shadows
Oh blonde giant

"I always thought it was called 5 o'clock shadow? said Jenny.

Pimbo smiled. "There's a new razor blade out called seven o'clock blade. You see how I've introduced the blade, depicted what a harvest-cropped field of stubble looks like – we could write all our little Haiku's on barber shop themes – so you see the project of ours could include these new innovations – does that satisfy you?"

A few days later, Len Tibbs, recent subject for Pimbo and Jenny's project, kindly sent them an old hairdressers' journal, the date of which seemed a bit obscure. Pimbo read through it avidly, picking out interesting facets of the hairdressing trade in other parts of the country. He chose the following for inclusion in the project thesis: The artistic chairman of Inter-coiffure John Oliver is making a return to his East Anglian roots by organising two days of teaching and shows in both Cambridge and Norwich. The last two years of his absence have been spent on the Continent giving demonstrations of hairstyling techniques. Open to all hairdressers. Tickets £10 each.

Hair fashions and styles at the moment, as approved by the following experts.

London. Vidal Sassoon cutting remains essential base for the new shaggy looks, both straight and permed, plus good conditioning.

Liverpool. Emphasis for next six months on curl, condition and colour from Anne Fergusson.

Stoke-on-Trent. John English. Advise strongly on cut and regular hair care.

Midlands. Student of the year Carole Nickson, foresees a move towards softer, curlier styles.

A Newmarket expenditure study, reveals that: British Teenage girls are big spenders. Three million girls between 12 and 18 have a combined spending power of £1,072 million a year.

Hairsprays are widely used; 12–13 year old girls spend 35 pence a month, as against 76 pence a month of the working 16–18 year olds.

In New York, Christine Valmy the hairstyling and beauty therapist is renting out space in her Fifth Avenue salon to three plastic surgeons and two dermatologists.

Then too, further snippets:

Joy Hathaway always wanted to be a hair-dresser and run her own salon. She began her apprenticeship way back in 1925. Fifty years later, she looks back, safe in the knowledge that she has achieved all the set out to do.

The early days were hard, but fun, working from nine in the morning until nine at night, every day, and 11 pm on Saturdays. All for 13/- a week!

She moved from salon to salon in learning every trick of the trade. "If I couldn't learn anything from a salon, I moved on to something more challenging" she said.

During those years, she entered competition after competition, winning scores of cups, silver plates, medals and certificates. A cabinet full of beautiful Dresden statuettes is proof of events she'd won. For 15 years she was president of the

Ladies Hairdressing Academy and has given demonstrations all over the country. "I've loved
every minute of it – it's been a lovely life!" was her
final word.

Fighting Home Hairdressers!

Salon owner, Emmanuel Rolf, has found the
answer to competition from home hairdressers,
which, is a growing problem in East Anglia.

He invites them to work in his salon on a
self-employed basis. They receive training and are
allowed to bring in their own clients on Mondays,
other afternoons, or evenings.

"Instead of setting their friend's hair at home,
they can do them in my salon. They bring in
clients who wouldn't otherwise visit a salon"

Should his scheme prove a success, he visual-
ises taking on others for training, or setting the
new hairdressers up in business. It was the only
way to take a swipe at home hairdressing and
bring into the salon those women who chose
because of low cost, to have their hair done at
home. Mr Rolf stressed, that they were super-
vised by a more experienced hairdresser when
doing colouring or more advanced techniques.

In a lighter vein, Pimbo chose. 'Hair–raising
Herbet', as follows. When it comes to customer
relationship, Herbert is tops. He inspects perms
and sets, checks hairdryers and generally flies
around the salon keeping clients amused.

He is the latest addition to the staff of the Hair
Time salon in Chippenham. He sailed in on the
breeze a few weeks ago and has proved a

tremendous success.

Herbert, however, is a stray homing pigeon and decided that Hair Time should adopt him. He was taken to a bird fancier who raced pigeons – but Herbert wouldn't settle down. Instead, he returned to the perms and hairdryers – a truly dedicated employee. As for the future, Herbert sees himself as a permanent fixture!

In conclusion, a temptation to the young bloods!

Australia

Young hairstylists required, must have ambitious outlook and be prepared for a change in lifestyle. 150 Australian dollars per week, guaranteed, but, 200 dollars per week easily earned with commission. Air fair paid to Australia and return fare to U.K. after two year contract period.

Next day the two youngsters visited their old friend Curly Northfield who was just back from doing his usual chores for the old age pensionsers. They showed him the project so far, the Haiku titbits, and the snippets from the Hairdressers Journal.

"Well done kids!" were his first words after having a long hard look at their work. "I should say you could call it a day now. Leave some of the current new barbers, until someone like you starts a new project in fifty years time. Don't worry about the Haiku lark, it affords a little light relief from cut-throat razor and leeches." He paused to study their young, anxious faces.

"Do you know kids, in London, barber shops are

used for painting exhibitions, poetry displays, framed pictures of boxers, racing men, horses, and what have you. You two kids have started a new trend, bless you both. Remember, our first idea of a time capsule? Well, I'm glad we changed it into a barber shop tales project and an interesting book for Cambridge people".

Jenny gave Pimbo an extra hug, she no longer worried about her first misgivings. "Miss English said she will go over our project for us, polish up the phrases, she thinks that we've set a good example to the school"

Pimbo nodded: It had been very hard work, the barbers had been wonderful in their help; some had said we had restored their faith in kids. Pimbo reckoned, that one day, when they were married with kids of their own, the likes of the old characters that frequented the barbers' shops and the barbers themselves, would all be gone, buried in a tome, entitled "Barber Shop Tales of Old Cambridge".

In conversation with Mr Robin Ivy concerning the Haiku writings originated by the Japanese barber, many years ago. Robin has given me a few excerpts from his booklet of Haiku snippets, entitled *Enigma: Poems for Meditation*. Here are a few:

It takes the fires
Of the Sun
To light the pale face of
the moon

Living too long
Is not a problem
For the Butterfly

A Blackbird's song
Has turned
The land into Summer

The large round orange
world
Of the Harvest Moon
Makes golden love in the
stubble

Sea Lavender is a lover
That dreams and longs
For the coming tide

Earth is a brief
Shadow
On the face of the Moon

There is no argument
About the resurrection
Of a Snowdrop

Pale delicate Sweet Peas
Jack Frost has come
To slit your throats

You can go mad
Trying to count
The stars

Wild Chamomile
The scent of dusty tracks
In a childhood summer

Mr Ivy's booklet, containing 34 poems, which was first published in London Poetry Quarterly, can be obtained from Mr Robin Ivy, 68 Rock Road, Cambridge.

They can be used as a help to creative writing for children!

Fred Unwin

I dedicate this book to Chelsea Robb. The young Poetess, (19 yrs) having nursed her mother through the pangs of a terminal cancer, has written this lovely poem. In the picture, Chelsea chooses a quiet spot in which to put down her thoughts.

For my mother, Sandra S. Robb, who is better by far than I could ever write . . .

The Word Mother

Everything about her is warm
like the wind in spring
on cold flowers.

Nothing she could ever do
could be wrong, or bad,
she is spring.

She is like fire to a frozen
tree, to help it bud.
She is rain to the seed
blooming in the earth,
teaching it to believe in the Sun:
in Greater Things, in Greater Beings.

How holy is her smile,
her touch is velvet.
Though sometimes we turned away,
we knew we needed them.

Think how she will listen,
when she is gone.
Think how she will listen,
in Heaven,
as our vision moves to her
in Heaven.
And our tears make rivers
for the spring.